THE COLOUR OF MY TEARS

MY JOURNEY OF HEALING

Morui Shoabi

Khumo Books
5448 Pennsylvania Close
Extension 5
Cosmo City
2188

info@kico.co.za

Ordering Information:

For details, contact the publisher at the address above.
Quantity sales only. Special discounts are available on quantity purchases by corporations, associations, and others.

First published in Johannesburg, South Africa by Khumo Books, 2020.

1st Edition Printed and bound by Khumo Books in South Africa, 2020.

ISBN: 9780620698252

TABLE OF CONTENTS

DEDICATION V

ACKNOWLEDGEMENTS VII

FOREWORD IX

INTRODUCTION XI

CHAPTER 1 1

There is an appointed time for everything

CHAPTER 2 15

Even though weeping may endure for a night joy comes
in the morning

CHAPTER 3 19

The journey of salvation

CHAPTER 4 33

I am saved

CHAPTER 5 43

The end of the sunshine state!

CHAPTER 6 57

One plus one is equal to two

CHAPTER 7 69
True healing requires a new foundation

CHAPTER 8 77
The mask of confidence

CHAPTER 9 87
Letting go of control, learning dependence and embracing vulnerability!

CHAPTER 10 97
Getting over the hurdles

CHAPTER 11 103
Getting rid of the skunk!

CHAPTER 12 113
I wish I had known him

CHAPTER 13 119
Veni vidi vici

CHAPTER 14 137
Detachment: although present, I was absent

CHAPTER 15 145
The state of sunshine

DEDICATION

I dedicate this book to:

Minister Shirley Mnisi, healer of the intangible things. Without whom, I might have remained a broken, scarred and voiceless child in a woman's body. You are a conduit of God's healing and an embodiment of God's love. Your passion and dedication to fulfilling your purpose is amazing.

Thank you for walking me through the path of healing. I pray that God will keep and protect you. May Abba Father continually favour you and shine His countenance upon you. I love you!

Ausi, my beloved mom, you taught me generosity and kindness. You took in those who were unwanted by society and gave them a home. You are my definition of what being good looks like. It's hard to comprehend how you single handedly raised two children, after Ntate's death. Thank you for raising us with such grace. I will forever cherish your memory. I am grateful for your life.

Ntate, we never met as you died too soon. I am here because you once lived. I hope we will one day meet in glory.

ACKNOWLEDGEMENTS

God, you are supreme. You are sovereign and eternal. Thank you, for healing and giving me eternal peace. My life is a demonstration of your goodness. This book showcases your greatness; your patience and willingness to work with us at our pace. You are a good Father. I belong to you and for that I am grateful. I adore you. I dedicate my life to glorifying your Holy name!

I owe gratitude to a lot of people who contributed toward shaping the woman I am; my late grandmother, Nkhono Mapuleng, the late Mannete Chaba, Isabel Walters, and Pastor Nonto Ndlovu.

I am grateful for my pastors, Apostle Eddie and Prophet Stella Phetla. I can't even begin to describe how much you do for me, thank you for your love and teachings.

To my family, you are my heartbeat. There are some experiences I wish I could erase, but they are the reason I have become the woman I am. God is redeeming us for Himself and is rewriting our story, giving us beauty for ashes.

I am indebted to my friends, Moruti Matshepo Mokobake, Mimi Mothupi, Vuyo Temba, and Siya Leshabane who took time to read and give valuable input on this book. Thank you so much.

I am beholden to the Gateway Church International family of churches, Moruti Sisinyana Setlogelo and the Letsiki's for your invaluable support.

Oesi Thothe, Nathi Mazibuko and Nsuku Nxumalo, thank you for your splendid work in editing this book. For every story there are back room heroes and heroines; for Khumo Books we have the brilliant Dineo Tlou, my business partner and Pako Tlou, the wind beneath her wings. I am grateful to both of you, let's impact the world for God.

Lastly gratitude goes to all my readers. Thank you for your support and helpful feedback. Your inspiration is the reason I write. I love you. Please keep it coming.

FOREWORD

By Shirley Mnisi

I marvel at God's pre-ordained plans hidden from us until the right moment. I love the way He gives us opportunities to witness these moments so that we may be left in awe.

Looking at how our paths crossed, I could not have imagined that it was for a bigger purpose. I met Shoabi (Morui) through Seipati. We were at a restaurant, having a casual meeting over lunch after an impactful weekend, of the Stellar School of Integrity camp.

My spirit leaped when I met her, I felt drawn to her. I started praying for her and I asked God to allow me to be a part of her life – as I knew I could minister healing to her.

I am grateful I walked with her through her journey of healing and restoration. It is amazing to see how she managed to allow her tears to colour her life. There were times, during our therapy sessions when I would want to cry with her, to hold her in my arms and assure her that God will heal her of her pain, but I couldn't. As it was important for her to confront her hurt and let the tears fall.

Her life is proof that human beings are not **'free from'** but are **'free to'**. We are **not free from suffering or hardships,** as we cannot control what happens in our lives, but we are free to **choose our attitude towards our fate.** We can influence the outcome through our choices and attitude. We are not what happens to us, but we are how we choose to respond.

I salute her for not choosing to be consumed by her pain and self-pity. For allowing herself to gain wisdom through her painful experiences.

She found her voice. She qualifies to be an advocate for the truth that there is meaning in every situation we go through and that the choices we make can lead us to victory. She expresses herself audibly through this book. This is a tool that can help us to stand up, dust ourselves and choose victory over victimhood.

INTRODUCTION

The first time I spoke publicly about some of the abuse I suffered in my past, was during a mission trip in Free State. When God told me that He wanted me to share my life story on a public platform, I was so nervous and uncomfortable, I could not keep any food down during that day. I was so worried about how people would react and how they would view me, that I missed the reason God wanted me to share my story.

When I eventually shared, many people responded to the altar call and many of them met with a counsellor for one-on-one prayer and counselling after the service. This response inspired me so much that I promised God I would use my story for His glory. This book is an expression of that promise. I pray that this book would encourage you to seek your healing and let go of the baggage you have carried all your life.

Writing this book was a mammoth task. I wanted to balance the act of telling you how I overcame my past without losing you in my misery. I particularly wanted to illuminate God's ability to redeem us for Himself and to cast a spotlight on His healing capacity. I hope I am able to do just that.

Although a large part of my emotional pain was healed miraculously, in other instances I had to go to therapy to get healing. I am grateful for the process, as it empowers you to heal yourself and others.

In writing this book, I deliberately broke a few language conventions and even used informal language in some instances. I did this in order to draw you into my world and to show you the richness of language use in South Africa. Where I have used non-English words, I have used footnotes to explain them. I pray that this book inspires you to seek your healing and that it allows you the freedom to free the child that has been crying within you.

There is no shame or condemnation in seeking help or speaking about your pain. Whatever you do though, don't camp around your pain or throw a pity-party. Seek help and work through it, so that you can live a great and fulfilled life.

YESTERDAY

CHAPTER 1

There is an appointed
time for everything

There is an appointed time for everything. And there
is a time for every [a]event under heaven.

Ecclesiastes 3:1 (KJV)

I imagine that if I was as flamboyant as The Great Gatsby; the opening line of my book might have gone something like, "she lived a charmed life, men followed her every move and women hung on every word she spoke."

Her beauty was unparalleled and suited her bold fashion expression. She had eyes that drew you into her soul and an endearing smile that made you feel special. Some said her intelligence was a result of choice genes, but some said she was a product of her studious grandmother's tutelage in all things concerning the world. While the legend of her intelligence is unconfirmed, we thoroughly remain captivated by her charm."

But mine is a story of an ordinary woman, who, after meeting Christ, became extraordinary. I would like to believe my story, in many ways, is no different from that of an average poor black child who grew up in 'ekasi[1]' under the apartheid laws.

My fondest memory is that of sitting under a tree where my best friend, Mogadi, would vividly tell stories of living stone characters. She was quite a narrator. I would spend hours listening to her. This is where I developed an appreciation of literature and storytelling. My childhood had a lot of beautiful moments in spite of itself.

I was born in 1975 on the 28th of March, on a beautiful Good Friday morning. To have Good Friday occur on the 28th of March is something

---

1 Ekasi is slang for township

that has happened three times in the 40 odd years of my existence. The year I was born, in 1986 and in 1997. This means I have had two perfect occasions, which I squandered to celebrate my birthday on Good Friday.

When I grew up, birthdays did not matter much. They served to mark an addition to your age. In the 80s we did not have a culture of celebrating birthdays as a family or as a community. We only ever made a big "huha" when one celebrated their 21st birthday.

That was the time when each young person looked forward to their birthday, as it meant a big celebration, where one would be given a key. An oversized decorative plastic key plated in gold or in silver written "21".

The key was presented to children who had kept themselves and had not done anything to disgrace their parents. Being given a key meant that your parents would allow you a degree of freedom from that day on. For an example, a girl would be allowed to introduce her boyfriend to the parents and vice versa. This meant it was no longer necessary to sneak around and stand on the corner of the street to get away from prying eyes. But you could visit your girlfriend at her parents' home and come through the front door. Anyhow, Soweto was cool like that.

I lost my father when I was four years old, but I remember him very well. As to whether that is a true memory or a figment of my imagination, I will never know. I am told that my father's death was caused by tuberculosis (TB). Something my grandmother was afraid would affect me when I became sickly during my teenage years. I, however, think that it is likely that my father died from Silicosis, a disease with similar symptoms to TB, as he was a miner.

When my father died, my paternal family accused my mother of having killed their son. This led to the separation of our two families. In our tradition children belong to the man, so my brother and I were separated from our mother and permanently relocated to Lesotho with my father's parents.

We lived for the Christmas holidays, when Ausi, our mother, would visit, bringing us new clothes and treats. No one explained to us why we saw our mother once a year. Furthermore, nobody explained, why I was suddenly uprooted from my paternal grandmother's house a year later. Separated from my brother and moved to my aunt's house.

It was during one of those Christmas visits that my mother "hatched" a plan to "steal" her children. In those days laws favoured men, which meant that my mother had no legal claim over us. Although we were her children, she was at the mercy of my paternal grandparents when it came to having access to us.

She was only able to smuggle one child out of Lesotho as my aunt got "wind" of my mom's plan. My aunt was then able to convince my brother to stay behind. That was the last I saw of my brother.

It helped that my brother and I were both born in South Africa, and only went to Lesotho after we were weaned off breast milk. This made it easy for my mother to get a copy of my birth certificate so that I could be enrolled in school.

During that fateful Christmas visit, a thorn pricked my mother while working with her sister in the maize field. That thorn turned out to be thornier than we had expected. At first, one leg was affected, then both legs became paralysed, thus causing her to lose the use of both her legs. There was no money for a wheelchair, so she had to be carried around.

My mother's family saw her illness as a spell of witchcraft from my father's family. They were convinced it was to avenge the death of their son. The result was a feud that saw two families hating and fearing each other for years. My brother and I were caught in-between, our allegiance swerved from one family to the other.

The combination of sub-human health services

that were available to black people and lack of technology back then, meant that the cause of my mother's paralysis was never found.

This is how living in Orlando East, Soweto started. That night when we arrived, I thought it was the most glamorous place I had ever seen. There were lights everywhere. This was until I saw the dirt, houses packed close to each other, each with a small yard having an unending line of shacks crammed on top of one another.

There was sewerage water everywhere and a bunch of dirty kids shouting and skipping the sewerage water as if that was normal. A few houses from my grandmother's house, was a huge garbage area, transformed into a hangout place at night.

We would make fire out of plastics and whatever we could find that was flammable. Although this was fun, the smell was so atrocious such that when we got home, we were subjected to bathing outside the house. My grandmother would say we were too dirty to enter her house.

We, of course would respond with opening the tap and allowing water to run over our feet. We would then proceed to smother ourselves with Vaseline and sometimes the Vaseline was used to cover the dirt. Not a great sight as you can imagine.

Our street like many other streets, was dirty and smelly, but no one seemed to care. On weekends there was competition between the loud music coming from different houses and the people speaking with each from across the street. A confusing place, for my small mind. The peaceful night died at the dawn of a new day.

I adapted quite easily. The following week, I started school and was taken to the second grade. I had to switch home languages and do Setswana as Sesotho was only available in Grade 5 at that school. This is how I ended up speaking Sesotho at home, Setswana in school, and a mixture of isiZulu, Tsotsi Taal and Sesotho on the streets. I became multilingual at a very young age, in fact it was weird to meet anyone who could only speak their home language in Soweto.

Life in Orlando East was a hive of activities. Mota Street nicknamed '36' because all the house numbers on that road started with the number '36', was lively. It was a popular street of sorts, loved by some and feared by others. While it was the home to fearsome gangsters and political activists of the time, it was my abode too.

If it was not the comrades who were burning an accused impimpi[2], it was the gangsters "knifing"

2 An impipi is a spy for the South African apartheid government

or shooting at each other. It was normal to pass a burning body on your way to school or for people to kill each other or have knife fights out of nowhere on the street. We got accustomed to death and human blood while we were still too young.

We became immune to violence and death; no danger seemed to stop us from doing what we liked. We were always running after one thing or the other. I loved playing outdoors, there was always so much to do. I liked the freedom of little supervision and the ability to explore while adults were at work. I never dared to venture far from home.

I suppose I was scared that I would be lost and never come back home, especially as stories of kids who never returned home were rampant.

My life was carefree until my mother became extremely sick. Her illness redefined our lives and forced me to mature at a young age. It is possible that my mother's illness revealed tensions that existed in the family. Either that or I became more attentive to my immediate environment. Living in a domestic war zone became my reality.

There was a clear sibling-rivalry in the house. Family members were forced to choose sides, otherwise you would be alienated. There was mistrust between my aunts and they would often accuse each other of various wrong doings. Children were often caught in-between and were sometimes forced to take a side.

I made sure that I was never part of it and avoided being drawn into it. My mother managed to stay out of it and played the peace-brokering part, perhaps because she had no way out as she was bedridden. I hated the conflict and the shouting matches that would ensue at the slightest provocation. Most times I would close my ears to drown out the noise or I will hum to myself.

This was in addition, to the conflict between my parents' families. The battle centred on my brother and me. On the one hand, I had to contend with my paternal family's dislike of me. Unlike my brother, I could not produce children to carry their name, therefore I was less important to them.

Although my aunts took care of me, they used every opportunity to remind me that my grandmother's house was not my home. This is why I have never felt like I belonged anywhere. I had no place I could call home. Although I called my granny's house, home, it never was my home it was a place where I lived.

Things worsened after my mother's death. Food was rationed and was often withdrawn as "punishment". When you did something wrong, you would be barred from eating. I soon learned to ignore my hunger and to survive on whatever I was given.

My mother's family was good at pretending. When no one was watching, they were the cruellest people imaginable but when we had visitors, their love for me would make even the most hardened of hearts, melt.

As I was not provided with most of the stuff I needed I worked throughout high school to support myself. From age fourteen until my matric year I worked at a bottle store (liquor store) every Saturday and during school holidays in December.

Working made it possible for me to buy my school uniform and the needed school supplies. I was even able to pay for some of my school trips. I got myself clothes and ensured that on those dark days where food was not provided, I could buy myself a kota (bunny chow).

In spite of all of this, I maintained my laughter. I used humour to mask my pain. My friends didn't know much about what was going on, away from their eyes. It was painful to share my experience because I believed it would not change my circumstances.

I presented a different picture of myself to the world. I pretended for so long that I began to believe the persona I had made up. In fact, this became so entrenched in my psyche, that I became the person I had created. The life I lived was packaged with a particular narration of conquests and adventures, concocted as part of my story. Just as I believed my own lie, those around me also bought into it. After years of pretending, I became the lie I invented. I could not remember my real identity, and neither could I separate the false from the truth.

When certain memories resurfaced later in life, I could not comprehend how they could have been part of my life, as the picture I had of my childhood could not reconcile with these memories.

TODAY

CHAPTER 2

Even though weeping may endure
for a night joy comes in the morning

I recently met a gentleman from South Sudan who had come to South Africa for a graduation ceremony. His story touched me so much, that to date I find myself praying for him, his family and the people of South Sudan. I was amazed at the ability of humans to continue living in spite of the difficult circumstances they face. Although he is separated from his family, he continues to work and study, improving his life, hoping that one day, he will have the life he dreams of.

This incident convinced me that our experiences inform who we become. I believe my life is a culmination of my experiences. Thus, the decisions I have made and who I have become have been framed by my past.

For me, there is nothing better than God, and nothing worth living for outside of God. I have seen God take me through what I thought would kill me. Therefore, I am certain that there is nothing that I can't overcome. This is why I live for God. My prayer every day is that I would glorify Him.

Indeed, I have made mistakes that have cost me, but I am grateful for each and every one of them, as they taught me good lessons. Certainly, they are lessons I would have preferred to learn differently. In spite of all this, God has been gracious to me.

I am often amazed by the passion I have for people. I shock myself when I see myself defending others to a point of burning my hands. It's things like these that make me see the powerful hand of God, as there was a time in my life, when I wanted nothing to do with people.

Presently I live a pretty good life and I am a pretty decent person, at least I think so. I am yet to achieve all my dreams and desires, but I am happily pursuing them. I live intentionally. I laugh a lot, especially at myself. I try to not take everything too seriously, as life is serious on its own. It does not need me to add to its intensity.

I rely on prayer to keep myself sane. I am one of those people who pray about everything and for everything. Prayer sustained me when I was uncertain of who I was and did not even understand what I felt half the time. To date, prayer remains the most important weapon I wield. I easily go to depths that few go to, as connecting with God is my lifeline.

My life is very simple. I don't worry about what I don't control. I try each day to focus on "the here and now" as yesterday is gone, I can only learn from it. I am grateful that I did not kill myself when death was all I could see and think of. I often find myself smiling for no other reason other than that I am alive. My joy is not a result of circumstances, it's a result of having a great relationship with God. I live in the consciousness that I am deeply loved by God; that I am secure in His hands and that He has nothing but good plans for my life and future.

I could talk about all my accolades and successes, but they are nothing compared to the salvation of Christ in my life. Indeed, this is not to say I don't enjoy the perks that come with the life I have been given. Every year I have been able to accomplish what used to be a childhood dream and to achieve goals that have enabled me to enjoy great promotion.

I am not yet as well travelled as I would like to be, but I have been to at least five continents of the world. Hopefully at the end of my life, I will have visited every country I have ever dreamt of and would properly earn the right to be called a "globetrotter".

Beyond this I pretty much live to fulfil my unwritten bucket list, which includes living the dream and overcoming things that used to scare me. Thus far, I have gone mountain climbing and I have done bungee jumping at Tsitsikama, the second tallest bridge in the world. One of these days, I would like to try sky diving and snorkelling.

I dance and sing the loudest, even though I can't sing to save my life. Only because I can. I know the secret of living a care-free life and it pleases me that I have not yet arrived at the place where I think I know all there is to life. This is my life!

CHAPTER 3

The journey of salvation

Psalm 121:5 The Lord is your guardian; the Lord is your shade at your right hand. (NABRE)

High School was difficult. Along the line, I lost consciousness of the care-free life I had led. I began to be aware of the emotional turmoil and misery I lived in. I spent a lot of time dreaming about a better life and wondering if it would ever come to pass. I spent my teenage years contemplating suicide, how I would do it and when was the best time to do it.

Admittedly, the pull to suicide was stronger after high school, it felt like I had come to the end of the road. It was painful to see people I went to high school with going to tertiary institutions while I stayed at home. It seemed my capacity to deal with life had been depleted.

We lived in a two-roomed house without a ceiling and thus hanging myself was not an option; as I could not reach the top with a chair. It also seemed like a cruel way to die. I therefore researched other ways of killing myself. I explored poison and an overdose, as these seemed viable. Fortunately, these methods were not immediately accessible at the time.

I am certain that if I had money, I would have died before I turned twenty. I was able to break the cycle of suicide, when it became clear, that dying would only serve the narrative of my family and not mine. I decided to live and work towards my dream life. I believed that being successful meant my family would one day come begging for my help.

In that way, I could finally prove to my family that I was worth loving and keeping. That I was not worthless, and I was not a "nothing". I also needed to prove wrong, everyone who had said 'I would never make it'. I, therefore, devised a plan to work hard to become the sole breadwinner for my family and die at the height of it.

I was not going to allow myself to live beyond forty. Forty was going to be the year, where I would finally rest in peace and find reprieve from my pain and difficulties. I believed that in death, I was going to find the ultimate victory. As I would have succeeded and died just as my family started depending on me. Leaving them hanging was going to be my ultimate revenge.

This was my perfect plan until God intervened. I was 27 when I received Jesus Christ as Lord and Saviour. Since then my life took on a different trajectory. It is not an exaggeration to say I would have died had it not been for the Lord. Even if I had 'chickened out' of suicide, I am convinced that the destructive habits I had cultivated, would have eventually led me to my untimely death. Either way, I was heading towards a cataclysmic end of my young life.

Before I was born again, I hated God. I was an Atheist who was convinced that black people were poor because they had bought into the lie of the Bible. I was convinced that God did not exist. I believed His existence was a lie meant to continue the subjugation of the black child. I suppose God pursued me the way He did because of this stubbornness. I was a modern-day Saul and I needed my own Damascus experience.

Two years before I met the Lord, I met Siya, who was to become a lifelong friend. I did not know she was born again at the time. Had I known that; I suspect I would have avoided further interactions with her.

According to Siya, we first met at a poetry reading session, where she was invited by a colleague who happened to be a friend of mine. While I don't recall this meeting much, I have a clear memory of meeting Siya at another friend's party, perhaps because she made a really bad impression on me that cemented my dislike of her. She came across as aloof, snobbish, and overly arrogant.

That night I decided, I was not interested in knowing her. Except that within a few weeks her name was suddenly popping up in all my conversations. Curiosity got me to rethink my prior decision. I determined to get a first-hand assessment of who she was. I guess I had a classic case of FOMO (fear of missing out).

Before long, I wrote a poem on sisterhood and sent it to a group of female friends, which included her. In truth, I was just being polite. It turns out the poem convinced her that I was worth inviting to coffee. I was reluctant at first, but eventually saw the light. We agreed to have lunch in Rosebank. That lunch turned into a whole afternoon and night out event. We discovered that even though we both had bad first impressions of each other, we in fact liked each other. We were cut from the same cloth, we echoed each other.

I discovered that just as I had thought the worst of her, she did not have a high opinion of me neither. She thought I was arrogant and self-centred among other things. For the first time, I had met someone who was not afraid to tell me what they thought. Our assessment of each other was probably correct, but it seems we were both comfortable with the bad traits we had. We were inseparable from that day on.

As I said I did not know that Siya was a born again Christian. I was also not aware, that at the time, she was going through some difficult issues with her faith. As we were both regulars at the hottest parties and clubs, almost every weekend.

When she one day suggested we go to church; I did not think much of it. I too went to church, once in every few years. Those few church attendances with Siya ignited the worst kind of criticism for God and Rhema Church. I did not know then, but this hard-line was what motivated Siya to start praying for my salvation earnestly.

Over the years Siya became more than a friend.

Her family adopted me into their lives, and I spent a few Christmases at her house. The Leshabane's are a close-knit family and being in their midst, one could not help but feel the love they had for each other.

I remember my first visit with Siya to Lebowakgomo. I had always thought Siya spoke a lot but that was before I met her family. I was unprepared for them; they really could talk. Their lounge was always filled with loud banter and hearty laughter. I loved Siya's mom. She was kind and loving. She had a way of reaching into your heart, that was unparalleled. Her love for her children radiated from within her eyes.

It was the ease with which the Leshabane's related that made me see what a family could be and what it meant to love each other. Siya's family had a Christmas culture which inspired me to eventually start something similar with my cousins. Before then, Christmas time in my family was just a day where nothing significant happened.

A year or so later Seipati entered the scene, she too would become a lifelong friend and sister. Just like Siya, when we met, I was not impressed with her. I thought she was loud and opinionated. I could not figure out why my friend had thought I was going to love meeting her. Just as it happened with Siya, in no time Seipati had become friends with all my friends. There was no conversation that happened without the mention of her name. History was repeating itself. So, it was time to check her out, I was curious why everyone couldn't stop talking about her.

The day I called her, she said, she was going to speak at a Land conference, this changed my perspective of her. That piece of information created a desire to meet her. Until that moment I had taken her for an "empty-headed" radio presenter. I am not quite sure how I had come to this conclusion but in all fairness, I probably took myself far too seriously than I should have.

The only saving grace is that Seipati also had a bad impression of me. I know one wrong does not cancel out the other, but it makes me feel better. Seipati thought I had pride and that I was arrogant. She believes, that had I died then, I would have contended for the throne of hell with satan. As sad and horrible as that sounds, now that I know better, I am inclined to agree with her.

I invited Seipati to an 'ancestral-honouring party' at my grandmother's house. She came along but refused to eat. I was insulted, especially when she told me she did not eat food offered to ancestors.

I am certain that had she not said she was speaking

at a land conference; I would have concluded that she was a lost cause and I would have thrown her out. Right at that moment, by declaring her Christianity to me, she was affirming her lack of progressiveness in my eyes.

Later that day, we drove to Kensington, where I lived. We spent that afternoon discussing books, politics, the land question, language, and the state of education in our country. We discovered we had read the same people and that we both had been influenced by similar authors. Although I was born & bred in Soweto and despised everything rural, she gained my respect that afternoon and nullified my stupid stereotypes about people who come from the 'rural' areas.

Little did I know that this was another Godly set up. Seipati and I used to have chats that lasted for hours and hours. These chats always ended up with Seipati talking about David. What I soon figured out is that the talk of David for some reason always led to how God used David. Her stories of David's exploits often culminated into a very detailed description of her own salvation. I should have been suspicious of this trend, but I was too immersed to notice.

It never mattered which topic we discussed, whether it be land, language or identity, it always boiled down to David and God. In those days, I was not a fan of God or the church, but I was curious about this God who spoke to her.

In all of my forced childhood church days, I had never heard anyone speak of talking to God, I wanted to know her God. Who was this God that spoke to her? How did He speak to her? If God could not be seen, how did He speak to her? These questions plagued my mind constantly. It's a good thing that google was not what it is today, otherwise I would not have gone to church.

I grew up in the Roman Catholic Church. The mass (church service) was only an hour long, but always seemed to go on forever. The Roman Catholic Church had prayers for everything, hence you needed to really know your Catechism. But my cousin and I never really learnt the prayers. We often got away with reciting the first few first lines and mumbling the rest.

I still remember the year we went through the Holy Communion classes. One day, the priest, Father Tlhagale, left us alone in class, to attend to an emergency. My cousin and I started telling other students that Christ was a Communist. We drew parallels between Carl Marx and Jesus Christ, in an attempt to prove that these two were the same. We did not see Christ as the son of God but only as a great philosopher. This offended the students, who reported us to Father Tlhagale. He was so upset that he threatened to disbar us from graduating. We were grateful that he took time out to pray and decided to hear us out before he made his decision.

Graduation was a license to officially partake in Holy Communion. As such, it was a big deal in my family. Not going through the ceremony, would have landed us in trouble. Our family had already planned a special Sunday lunch, and my white dress was ready, a dress specially bought for this occasion. We had to apologise and renounce our statements as the work of the devil. Our punishment was to go to 'Confession', which we thought was fun.

We each went into the confession room and our penance was a recital of a few prayers. But instead of reciting prayers we went outside the confession room, bent as if praying and started chatting. We would only stop talking when we heard footsteps. We would then loudly recite a few lines of the different prayers holding the Rosary. We were ridiculously naughty. For us, church was a place we were forced to go to and therefore a place where we coped by breaking rules.

This is why it was a big deal for me, when I asked Seipati for a bible. I had never owned a bible and I didn't know where I could get one. I think I was also a bit embarrassed to go looking for one. Well that was the beginning of a great journey. What I did not know at the time was that I would grow to love the bible the way I do now. Nothing gives me more nourishment than the word of God. Every year I read the bible page to page at least twice.

BETWEEN YESTERDAY AND TODAY

CHAPTER 4

I am saved

Now that you know Siya and Seipati, it's worth back tracking for your understanding. You see, before Seipati came with all her stories of David and how she got saved, Siya had already dunked me deeper into salvation than I knew. As I said in the previous chapter, I did not think much about her suggestion to go to church.

Especially as the suggestion came from one of our drunken stupor conversations. In those days, our conversations were very deep, especially when drunk. In case you are not from South Africa or you belong to the generation of properly written English, 'deep' in street language basically means heavily philosophical or spiritual.

On the day, the talk of church crept into our conversation, we were in one of our favourite hangout places in Melville. I was feeling indulgent and a bit generous when Siya gave me a whole speech about how once in a while we needed to get a different perspective on things, hence the need for church. Therefore, when I agreed to go to church with her, I had no idea that she actually meant it.

It turns out, Siya being Siya, was pretty serious about church. This is how I found myself back in church after 10 years or so of not having been there. The last time I had been to church was in Standard 8 (Grade 10).

When I stopped attending church regularly, school was my excuse. Back then we always had Saturday classes to 'catch up' on different subjects. In addition to my classes I had special mathematics lessons. This meant that my Saturday was taken up with studying.

I, therefore, reasoned with my grandmother that I needed Sunday to do my laundry. Plus, I was becoming politically conscious, and church was not a place to go. There were a lot of opinions floating around that were critical of God and the church. All these issues helped me make a case against going to church. My grandmother made me try out the Dutch Reformed church, as it was the church my mother preferred.

I suppose she thought that going to a church that my mother used to love would help, but even that could not do much to change my apathy. Thinking about it, it's funny that church was so important to my grandmother, yet she never attended much of it.

Going to church that Sunday morning, I had no idea what to expect. Firstly, I did not expect to be confronted by a place which housed different nationalities and races on any particular Sunday. Secondly, I was a bit thrown off by the smiling faces and friendly handshakes, from people I did not know. Thirdly I did not expect a white pastor to be willingly followed by so many black people. "Did these people not understand we had just won against white domination?" I used to wonder.

Lastly, I had not expected such a colossal structure to be a church. I was so shocked, that I concluded that it was all a Ponzi scheme. I gave Siya such a hard time about having a white Pastor, after church. I even did a calculation of how much the church made from all the people I presumed to be gullible. Especially when I heard they had multiple services on any particular Sunday.

I counted the number of seats and estimated an

average offering of R5 per person, the total convinced me that church was a business set out to make the top guy, who happened to be white, rich. I was sure that these people were being duped out of their hard-earned money. Especially when I saw my logical and no-nonsense friend giving R20 during offering. Back then R20 was a lot of money, and I could not figure out how she would give that much to a church that clearly did not need money.

I could not wait to tell her about her foolishness. I could not understand why she woke us up so early and took us on an unending journey, from Soweto to Randburg just for that bubble. I am pretty sure I did not even hear the message. My heart was calloused and hardened to God. But God, being gracious and merciful, did not cease to pursue me. Soon enough Siya's prayer for God to help me see the light was answered through Seipati.

After a few months of hearing of David, his exploits, and the God that spoke to Seipati, I was ready to find out if this God was for real. This is when I asked Seipati for her old bible. I asked her for a bible at the beginning of 2002. That year, my birthday was on the eve of Good Friday. My friends and I had planned a big party at Sparks Gallery in Norwood. Back then I was known for being the life of the party and throwing hot parties. It was no different that year.

The 28th of March 2002 was a night of great ambiance. The art was something to behold, the music and food was amazing. At the end of the night I was content and smug. I had pulled off yet, another fit. After my party, Seipati, Thabiso and I drove to Lesotho for a performance Seipati had. In those days, I really liked going along with her and Thabiso, although I am not sure why, as crowds were really not my thing.

As always Lesotho was great fun. Unfortunately, on our way back, we were involved in a car accident. We had a tyre burst that resulted in the car overturning and rolling a few times before it landed in someone's farm. None of us had had a safety belt fastened.

Coming out unscathed, from that wreck, was surreal. When I came out of the car Seipati was bleeding and walking around the car praying. Thabiso was still in the car. I looked around to see our belongings scattered in the farm and it seemed as if the car had shrunk. I was under shock, but I had a peace I could not explain. For the first time in my life I knew that God truly existed. All the questions or doubts I had ever had about His existence were solved. God used that accident to convince me of His existence.

After the accident, I kept asking myself if I now knew that God existed, why did I not believe in Him? I wanted to know what stopped me from being saved. I then started researching the meaning of salvation. I was seriously considering Christianity. Although I still mocked it, as I thought it was ridiculous. I especially could not understand how one could live without sex until marriage.

I also did not get the idea of marriage, what if I did not want to get married? To me marriage was slavery. To think that I would be required to leave a club early so that I could go to church the following day, was also a bit crazy. I thought that so many things about Christianity did not add up, but I could not let go of God. So, I continued to read up on Christianity.

As I was researching and dealing with my findings, I would share my thoughts with Siya. She would laugh at me. Little did I know that she was praying about everything I told her, refuting and casting down every argument I had. Heaven and earth were in an unwavering partnership for my salvation. In July 2002, four months after our car accident, I accepted Jesus Christ as my Lord and Saviour, at home. By then I knew the sinner's prayer by heart, as Seipati had told me her salvation story in detail many times. However, I was still not sure if I really was saved.

Hence a week later, I responded to an altar-call at Rhema Bible Church. I wanted to make sure that I was truly born again. Since then, my life has never been the same. It seemed no amount of reading could have prepared me for salvation. My heart was completely gripped. I disappeared from my normal scenes. I could not get over God. I read the bible from Genesis to Revelation. I attended every prayer meeting I could find and attended every training course made available at church. As a result, I was no longer available for parties.

My inner man changed without me being conscious of it. It helped that a few months before I got born again, I had moved from Kensington to Sundowner, which was far from everything. This made it easy for me to disappear into the new world of salvation and to allow a new culture to be birthed in me.

It was only after a year, that I emerged out of my cocoon. I began to tell people of my salvation, including those who used to be in my inner circle. It took me that long to have the courage to tell my friends that I had changed. The good thing though is by then I was strong enough to deal with their responses.

Some friends who were into politics said I had betrayed the struggle; while others thought I had become a crazy fundamentalist. Either way, I did not care, I was sold out to Christ and I was not about to change my mind. I lost about 98% of my friends which was pretty difficult. Especially losing friends, which had been there for the greater part of my life. I am glad that Seipati was there to disciple me and to help me overcome the negative reactions. Siya remained constant in the process of my journey. It seems while praying for me, she ironed out her issues with God.

These two women held up my arms while I figured myself out and grew in maturity. My whole life changed. I reiterate, nothing could have prepared me for salvation, not even the research I made before I accepted Jesus Christ as Lord and Saviour. I had no clue what the impact of inviting an eternal God into my life, would be. My focus and my reason for living changed. Most importantly, the things I used to deem necessary became trivial.

I went on a mission to evangelize everyone I came across. My intentions were good, but my methods were sometimes very unpleasant. I shoved salvation into people's throats most times. I was forceful in the worst of ways.

Even so this was a great training ground, I learnt a lot about evangelism in that season. A year later while, I was an 'Effective Evangelism' student, I met a gentleman I had once shared the gospel with. Hearing how I terrified him into getting saved sobered me up. It taught me to share my faith in a more pleasant and considerate manner. I learned that salvation is a choice and thus needs to be presented as such.

CHAPTER 5

The end of the sunshine state!

———

I threw myself into a life of salvation with all I had. It was not comparable to anything I had ever known. There was a call to let go of myself and give myself completely to God. I had found freedom and I wanted it to filter into every part of my life. My relationship with my family was restored. Parts of my heart that were previously closed, opened up to them.

Along the line, I had completely cut-off my family. However, after I became born again, I reopened the communication lines. I resumed helping financially where I could. I let go of anger and began to extend kindness to my family. I also realised that with every success and promotion, I had developed pride, specifically towards my family. This was propelled by the fact that I had succeeded in spite of them. God then took me through a long process of dealing with that pride filled heart of mine.

I excelled in my pursuit of God and little by little, I regained my reason to live. I was delivered from depression and suicidal thoughts. Even though by the time I got born again, I was no longer convinced that killing myself was a viable option, I still had obsessed with death. Death ceased being my number one favourite topic.

I did not realise, however, that dealing with the junk that had 'soiled' my soul (mind and heart) was my responsibility. I thought that being born again meant that my soul was automatically cleaned and reset on a new path.

Furthermore, I expected miracles for everything I did not want to deal with. I had lived a difficult life therefore I wanted an easy life in salvation. I wanted things to happen without my input. Much like how we sometimes expect things to be different in our lives without making any effort to change.

Anyhow, I started doing ministry soon after my salvation, which helped with my spiritual growth and maturity. I ran a home cell after being born again for a year, became a board Member of Mannete Chaba Eagles Ministries and became her ministry's Marketing Manager. In 2005, I co-founded an organisation called Rona Regeneration Project, an NGO that launched the Pantsula 4 Christ Outreach Ministry in 2006.

My life was great until January 2016, when I met a prophet whom I thought was weird at the time. He gave me what seemed like a 'zany' prophecy. I thought he was odd, probably because I subconsciously wanted to discredit him, but I sensed that he was genuine.

At the time, I really thought he was crazy, as he told me I had a lot of emotional pain that I had blocked. I flat-out denied what he said because I was convinced that I had dealt with all my past emotional pain. He responded by saying that although I had learned to live with my pain, I had not dealt with it. That pain still imprisoned me.

In spite of my disagreement, I could not refute what I sensed in my spirit, so I promised to pray about his prophecy. I prayed but I heard nothing. His prophecy had me asking a lot of questions, like what pain was he talking about and where was this pain hidden?

When I did not hear from God, I let go of it. Clearly patience was yet to manifest in my life. I don't know why patience was a struggle for me. Especially since driving on Johannesburg's roads every day, which I did, required an excessive amount of patience, tolerance and love.

Just as I thought I had enough unanswered questions in my life. A few weeks later I received yet another wacky prophecy, from a completely different person. It felt like God was out to get me. The prophecy spoke of my bright future. However, the prophet declared that before I got there, God was going to first remove the 'dross and the tin' in my life. He said that this was going to be a painful process.

Yet again I was confused and frustrated. I was not sure what he was talking about, but my spirit compelled me to give attention to what he was saying. I was frustrated at God for speaking to me in what seemed like riddles. I prayed without much success, so I decided to forget about the prophecies and live my life. I concluded that God would tell me what he wanted to tell me when He was ready.

Around July of the same year, I lost my cousin tragically. During the week, while we were preparing for his burial, I started having feelings of great despair, I felt empty. It was like there was a dark deep hole within me. I felt deeply ashamed, as if people could see my nakedness. It felt like my life had no meaning, that I was living a lie. I wanted to end it. I could not understand these feelings. The last time I had felt anything remotely close to how I felt, was when I still suffered from depression.

In a matter of a few days I went from being 'the talkative worker-bee' to being quiet and moody. While I was sad that I had lost my cousin as I could not get over the senselessness of his death, I knew something else was the source of these feelings. Yet I could not figure it out. It was while chatting with Minister Shirley on WhatsApp that it became apparent that I was dealing with the impacts of a resurfacing memory that had been suppressed.

Try as I might, I could not remember the experience but what I felt was real. This is how I got to agree to go for counselling. Although I was desperate, I was still skeptical. I had done a lot of counselling in my early 20's with very little results. It was suggested that I try Logotherapy, a meaning-centred therapy. Although it was explained at length, I doubt that I was listening much. I honestly don't think I was convinced it would work, but I was anxious enough to check it out. I would have preferred a magic wand, to help me get the pain miraculously expunged.

I was surprised to discover that the commitment to seek help would give my suppressed memory permission to resurface. One Friday morning, while driving to work, the lost details of my childhood materialized in my mind. I was in shock. Tears started flooding my face. I have never felt such pain, it was worse than anything I knew.

To suddenly have this horrendous memory forming part of my life experience was gut-wrenching. Thinking of it now, I cannot imagine how I must have looked, crying on the road. Thank God for a car with tinted windows right? By the time I got to work, I had found a way to keep a semblance of dignity and keep the storm of tears in abeyance.

Throughout the first two hours of my workday I kept coming back to that memory. I felt so much sadness, but after much prayer I was able to focus on my work. Little did I know that I was just postponing the inevitable.

Friday evening, I came back home, fixed something to eat and situated myself on the couch in front of the TV. The plan was to have a quiet evening in the company of all the TV series I had missed during the week. As it would happen before the night was up, something in my beautiful selection of TV programmes, triggered my memories. And for the rest of the evening the tears I had suspended earlier on came tumbling down in torrents.

The tears were unbearable, but this time around I gave them freedom to reign. I cried myself to sleep and woke up only to find myself crying again. I cried so much that I began to laugh at the ridiculousness of the whole situation.

By Saturday afternoon I felt renewed. I still did not know how to deal with the memory that had crept into my life, but I felt better. This is why I decided to keep my resolve of going to therapy the following week, even though I now knew what the cause of the emotions I felt was.

Monday came and I started being anxious about the planned therapy. I had initially made an appointment for a morning session but decided to move the appointment to the afternoon. This was after I had a vision of myself crying uncontrollably. I did not want to have a repeat of the experience I just had the week before.

Driving to therapy on that Wednesday was torturous. I was having second thoughts, wondering if I really wanted someone fishing in my head. I was already thinking about whether I was ready to bare it all to someone I barely knew. But I drove on, nevertheless. My desperation coerced me to keep driving. I was frightened of therapy, but it seemed as if I had no other choice, as I did not know how else to deal with everything on my own.

I prayed for myself to remember why I was going to therapy. I asked God to help me to open up and to make the best of the experience. I was eager for a change and was tired of carrying the pain.

Therapy that day was difficult, because it took me back to that hot summer day when I was raped. I was nine years old and had been visiting relatives in Limpopo. One day while we were left alone, I was raped by a group of boys. I recoiled when I remembered. The details came crashing into my mind and I was overcome by the horror of the experience. I had never felt so helpless. I must have blacked out during the experience as there were parts I could not remember.

The pain brought by the memories ripped me apart, l felt like my insides were torn off. I wept uncontrollably. I was glad I obeyed the Holy Spirit and did not put on make-up that day. I had never felt so much anger, I kept asking myself, "how could they do that to me and why did they do it?"

I don't know why the mind feels the need to ask questions in such moments. Perhaps it's the need to comprehend what is overwhelming, the need to find answers, to understand the cause of brutality or to find justification, I don't know.

The worst part was remembering that my family did nothing. They behaved like nothing had happened and life continued as usual. This broke me. My heart was in tatters. I understood for the first time, why I never thought I mattered or that my feelings mattered. It seemed like my family stood on the side of my perpetrators. I was left thinking what happened to me was my fault, that I deserved it and was being punished for something unknown to me.

I felt robbed and violated. I was angry at my family for not doing anything. I felt exposed and unprotected. How could those who were meant to protect me do nothing? In that therapy session, I dug into my pain. I dealt with the innocence I lost, the anger and hatred I felt against my perpetrators and my family. There was so much anger towards my mom.

While my mom was not with me in Limpopo, I had expected her to seek justice for my hurt, but she did not. Until that memory, I had held her in high esteem. But after I remembered what happened, I did not know what or how to feel about her. I was so disappointed in her. All my life she had been my measuring tool of goodness and kindness. I left therapy relieved of my pain but unsure of what to do with all that was unearthed.

After therapy I was drained but had been freed

from all the anger and resentment I carried for years. The decision to release and forgive all the people who had wronged me, both the perpetrators and my family, freed me.

I understood that forgiving them did not excuse them of their actions, but liberated me from the 'prison of unforgiveness' that their actions had locked me in. I felt lighter than I had ever felt in my entire life. I was surprised that I had carried so much weight all along. What I was unsure about, though, was how to feel with all these people I had forgiven. The realisation that the absence of hate and anger did not equal love, was fascinating for me.

We take it for granted that we can move from resentment and anger to love. The truth is, the soul needs time to adapt to the new. This process cannot be hurried. It must be allowed to take its course. My responsibility was to learn to live a life that was without anger and hatred and to teach myself new responses. This meant embracing those moments when my own reactions would scare or surprise me, because they revealed a person I did not know. This I think was the hardest part. It often left me uncertain, but it was also the most exciting thing.

Although I dealt with being raped on that day, it took months for me to come to a place of complete healing. Indeed, I had forgiven my mom, but still I did not know how to feel about her until a few months later.

One afternoon I was driving home playing R&B music, my playlist came to a song by Paul Young, 'Wherever I lay my Hat'. While listening to this song I remembered that my mother used to love it. On that day, I paid attention to the lyrics, they were so sad. I began to wonder what state of mind my mother was in to have loved and related to that song.

I had always assumed that my mother died while she was in her forties but somehow that did not ring true that day. The thought of her age kept playing in mind until I called my Mamkhulu (aunt). I asked her how old my mom would have been if she was alive? I realised, for the first time, that she was only twenty-nine when she died, which meant she would have been twenty-seven when I was raped. I was so shocked.

I had been so angry and disappointed that my mom did nothing, that I hardly thought about what she must have gone through when she found out I was raped. I could not imagine what she must have gone through in her own life. By age 27 she was widowed, a paraplegic, unemployed and unable to take care of herself let alone her children.

At 27 she had to deal with an accusation that she had killed her husband and was left with two children she could not support. One child was taken from her and she had not seen him in three years; and on the other hand, her daughter had been raped while she was supposed to be in the protective custody of those she trusted.

For the first time in my life, I saw my mother as a person. I saw her as a young woman who, I imagine, had barely figured out herself when she was left with this big responsibility. I also remembered that I never visited Limpopo again after that incident, which was possibly her way of protecting me.

Seeing her this way changed my perspective. I understood that she possibly dealt with my situation the best way she knew how. Although it was not how I would have dealt with things, when she was 27, her world was completely different to the one I lived in. Although I was mature at twenty-seven, I was barely equipped to deal with what she had to deal with.

This brought so much healing to me. That day my mother stopped being a villain and became a noble character. I now have great respect for my mother. I don't know how she managed to be kind and generous in spite of her circumstances. She was a strong woman. She could have become bitter, but instead she brought hope to a lot of people. She took care of children whose mothers could not care for them. She fed people who had no one to feed them and still managed to mother me the best way she knew how.

I remembered all these things and that my mother had time to listen to me after school. She knew my favourite songs. She would call me to come and listen, when my favourite song played on the radio. That day I made peace with looking like my mother, I embraced it. I remembered so many positive things that she had done for me. Pain had clouded my perspective.

She had entrenched a love for plants in me. Yet for so many years I had hated anything to do with plants or gardening. I now have pot plants in my house and nurturing them has been a part of the healing process.

I no longer had the need to divorce myself from my mother and from everything that she stood for. This brought so much joy to me. I was amazed at how much making peace with the memory of my mother, allowed me to embrace all that I had hated about myself. I used to dread hearing the old granny next door, calling me by my mother's name. Our strong resemblance always confused her into thinking that I was my mom. I had the ugly job of reminding her that my mother had passed away all the time.

In finding healing I discovered that I had empathy

for my elderly neighbour, and I did not mind that I confused her. I no longer hated correcting her. I was happy to be my mother's child, grateful that I am credited with some of her great qualities.

CHAPTER 6

One plus one is equal to two

———

To all who mourn in Israel, he will give a crown of beauty for ashes, a joyous blessing instead of mourning, festive praise instead of despair. In their righteousness, they will be like great oaks that the Lord has planted for his own glory.

(Isaiah 61:3 NLT)

Doctors know, priests know and those who were ever victims know, freedom is not freedom when you have never known what freedom is.

The law of gravity dictates that what goes up must come down. Similarly, the law of trauma dictates that all that is suppressed eventually must resurface. All it takes is the right trigger.

When I went to therapy to deal with the rape memories, I did not know there were other things I had suppressed. One by one, horrific memories came tumbling down, or rather up. I had always thought I had lived a care-free life. I thought that the only scars I had, were that I had grown up poor and that I was an orphan. It turned out that this was a lie. I could not resolve the life I had convinced myself of and the actual truth of my life.

I recollected so many incidents that happened over the years. I remembered that I was often left alone, while sick. As a child I was sickly and would often miss school for days or weeks at the time. I suspect my family must have grown tired of my illness, especially as healthcare for black people was atrocious. The economic conditions did not make it easy for blacks to care for their families. As such one could not be away from work because they were sick or had a sick child.

I can vividly remember one particular day, I must have been in Grade 8 or 9. By then my mother was late, I lived with my granny and aunts. I had been sick and bedridden for a week or so. My family thought it was all right to leave me with a three-year-old cousin who could barely take care of himself. Once in a while I could walk around the house leaning on walls to make him food, but I spent my time mostly sleeping. This was fine, until one specific day, when things did not go well.

Home was a two-roomed brick house that had an additional room built out of corrugated iron, which we called a 'veranda'. We had several families living in the yard with us. We shared a communal toilet. I must have been too pressed that day, as I had to walk to the toilet. Halfway there I blacked out and fell. When I re-gained consciousness, Mokholo, my cousin was staring at me looking scared. My disabled neighbour was calling out my name from his yard. I tried crawling to the toilet but could not make it. I blacked out again. I woke up in bed, it seems my neighbour helped to take me back to the house. This in itself was a great feat, as he could barely walk on his own.

This memory 'replayed' in my mind for days on end. I tried to switch it off, but it would not go away. I was shocked at the cruelty of it all. I kept wondering what I had done to make my family hate me so much. Eventually I decided that this was a defeating thought and I let it go. But as soon as I did that, other ugly recollections came up.

I remembered all those days I went hungry because someone thought it was okay to hide food. I recalled, how I would pretend to be full at school, to avoid questions of why my aunt, who was in the same class with me, had money for food and I did not. I hated the constant questions asked, like, why she was always going on trips and I couldn't. Most times my family gave my aunt money and would tell her to say the money came from her boyfriend. However, she found joy in telling me the truth and that gnawed at me. I hated my family and their lies.

As the memories surfaced, I could not reconcile the anger I felt with my faith. How did I live all these years raising my hands towards heaven when there was so much underlying pain I did not even know existed? I thought I had dealt with my family; that I had forgiven them, but it was apparent that I had not fully done so.

I discovered the truth of the prophecy I got earlier in the year, that I needed to deal with my childhood trauma. The prophet had specifically said that although I had learned to live with my pain, I had not overcome it. He said I had so many walls that caused double standards in me. That line alone suddenly made so much sense.

I also noticed a myriad of complications of having had so much abuse in my life. I had developed so many walls and coping mechanisms that it was hard to say which part of me was real and which wasn't. I understood why being told to 'be me' or 'do me' had often seemed so irritating. I had not known who I was or worse, which parts of me were real. Furthermore, I did not know which parts of me were a result of trying to cope with the reality of pain.

I struggled with so many basic concepts that formed part of being human, *one of them being love.* I had no idea of what love was. As I had equalled love with pain, rejection, hurt and obligation.

I had attached so many conditions to love, that it was absurd. Love for me, had to be earned. Whenever love was given to me, I would work hard, just so that I could deserve it. This caused me so many problems because when I was not expected to perform, I would become awkward and uneasy.

I also realised I did not truly trust the love of God, which came without conditions. It shocked me when I realised that my great life of salvation was based on working to earn what was freely given to me. It made sense that God kept telling me to trust Him at every turn. No matter how much God tried to show me my lack of trust, I would often minimise it to me not having trusted Him in a particular area. That was easier to deal with, rather than the fact that I did not trust God in entirety.

I woke up to the revelation that I had an overall issue of trust. Something central to my inability to fully accept that the love of God was freely given to me. I had such a perverted notion of love. Realising that I struggled with both God's and man's love, made me grasp that I also had issues with human love. I often wondered what people meant when they said they loved me. I questioned what they loved in me. Only because I did not think I was deserving or worth loving.

This filtered to romantic love. I had never been in-love in the true sense of the word. Yes, I have had great relationships and yes, I thought I had fallen in love a few times. However, I had never fallen in love in the true sense of the word. As in, I had never lost myself in someone.

I had just started dating someone and all these realisations made me to instantaneously loose interest. I was a forty-something-old woman trapped in the mind of a broken child. I found it hard to trust what I was feeling, as I needed to peel off so many layers to get to the real me. I also had to break walls I had built to protect myself; walls I did not even know existed until that very moment.

I thought I was going to suffocate with pain. I took my journal and started writing, in between the tears. I cried for the child that was wronged and broken until she was a shell of herself. I cried for the woman who was left with footprints of pain, old and stubborn scars, the woman who struggles to live well today.

It was in that moment of confusion that I cried out to God. Although there were still many things, I questioned about God, He was the only thing I was sure of. I knew I could trust His word, so I called out to Him. In my tears, I felt the light flood my heart. I had never experienced the love of God the way I did on that day. I kept hearing the following lines from John Legend's song, 'All of Me' play in my mind.

'Cause all of me
Loves all of you
Love your curves and all your edges
All your perfect imperfections
Give your all to me
I'll give my all to you
You're my end and my beginning
Even when I lose I'm winning

Cause I give you all of me
And you give me all of you, oh
How many times do I have to tell you
Even when you're crying, you're beautiful too
The world is beating you down, I'm around through
every mood"

When I heard these words, I crawled into the arms of my Father. This song captured what I needed to hear and receive from God. I took comfort in His strength and wept as He rocked me. God loved me, in spite of all my imperfections. He loved me with all the scars I had. He called me beautiful and above all, He wanted to heal me. He wanted to give me all of His good and exchange it for the bad I had. I was overwhelmed with love.

This song opened me up to working through the self-hatred I had, all the emotions of unworthiness and the ugliness I felt. I wanted to work through my fear of attaching to people, opening my heart to love. I let go of the fear of being vulnerable and of the future. I understood that even though there was no guarantee that my life's path would be smooth, God was with me and would never forsake me.

That day I mourned the girl I lost, forgave myself

and let go of the hatred I felt towards myself. I forgave my family for everything they did and released all the anger and resentment I felt towards them.

I determined to work through every insecurity, every negative word ever spoken, and every ugly memory I had. Negative words are damaging. They create a pattern of ugliness in our lives. This ugliness becomes an invisible cloak that begins to inform your life and to determine who you become.

The scars of negative words are incomprehensible, their impact is invisible to the naked eye. Somehow a physical scar is easier to heal and treat. However, an invisible scar is more challenging to heal because you may not even be aware that it exists.

If negative words can be this powerful, imagine how much impact and transformation, positive words can bring in your life. Not only do they serve to build on the foundation that God has built on, but they serve to reaffirm your identity and establish you as a force to be reckoned with. Positive words are powerful. They create an enabling atmosphere. I can testify to this truth.

This is how I began my journey of healing. I doubt I would have chosen it, if I had not discovered the extent of the harmful baggage I was carrying. I did not know that healing meant I would have to face the horrible things done to me and the horrible things I had inflicted on myself in an attempt to deal with my pain.

My therapist encouraged me to keep a journal of my feelings and experiences of the healing process. This journal has helped me gain perspective and above all, get to the answers locked within me. I was amazed at how easy it was to not pay attention to my emotions or myself, as I struggled with being present.

The journal became a mirror that helped me look at myself and decide on what to pay attention to. It also helped me to see myself the way God sees me. I needed to make certain confessions that counteracted all the negative words I had believed.

The first set of confessions came from my therapist and then I took the lead to create a few more for myself. I learnt that you do confessions, until they become truth that is embedded in you and until they inform your thinking.

I am grateful for life. Life is a beautiful thing. It is amazing to serve or give as a response to the blessing you have been bestowed with, instead of giving out of obligation. Every day I wake up with the assurance that I am deeply loved by God, that He values and approves of me. This has changed my prayer life and has shifted how I utilise the gifts He has given me.

I used to be afraid of using my gifts and preaching, I did not want to make mistakes and incur the wrath of God. However, knowing that I am accepted and approved regardless of the mistakes I may make, has been freeing.

CHAPTER 7

True healing requires
a new foundation

Recently, I was reminded of a friend who used to say that he did not want to marry a beautiful woman, but he wanted to marry a woman who knew she was beautiful. His theory was that a woman who was beautiful but did not know it, would burden him with insecurity.

I had never thought of myself as less than wonderful and this has always been the perception of myself. Hence, I understood why my friend would want a woman who thinks she is beautiful. What I did not realise, though, was that the wonderful me was just a persona put together as a cover up of a broken woman riddled with issues, one of them being *shame*. Shame was an invisible cape that caused me to want to hide. I did not want to be seen. I hid myself because I thought shame was written on my forehead.

Each time I looked at people I thought that all they saw was shame. I was convinced that my history was visible to all. In my mind, I carried a billboard written, *'molested, raped, verbally and physically abused'* *etc.* This is how I determined to hide my true self and created a persona that was confident and nonchalant. I was once told that had I died before I got born again, I would have contended for hell with satan because of pride. Yet in truth, pride was primarily a robe and a guise hiding all that was wrong within me.

I spent some time thinking about where so much shame came from and found out it started when I was four and was molested by an uncle. When you are a child, are made an accomplice to your own violation, and are scared into keeping quiet, you think that you are the cause of what happened to you, especially as you do not have the vocabulary to explain what happened in the first place. All I felt was shame about my nakedness and my body. Being naked was no longer an innocent thing to be enjoyed, it was something to be ashamed of.

I did not want to be seen naked, I wanted to cover myself. I became uncomfortable when people looked at my body. I suspect the need to hide started there. To date I occasionally struggle with my body, but I am getting better. A lifetime of belief cannot be addressed in one day, this is why I continue to preach to myself that my body is not a source of shame. I will do this until this truth is established in my life.

I was ten when I started wetting my bed without an explanation. Another experience that cast a huge black cloud over my life. At first the elders thought I was being naughty. In an attempt to mitigate the situation, I was told to stop drinking liquids at night. When that did not work, the constant beating and name calling started. I got into a habit of closing my ears or singing when the shouting started, but this only invited more beatings. I got beaten so frequently I stopped crying.

I was taken to a Sangoma to "heal" me. She gave me vile medication that I could not keep down. When that did not work, my family tried every single remedy they could think of. Some of these included eating a rat and drinking detestable herbs, but the problem continued. No matter how hard I willed the problem away, nothing ever changed.

I was grateful and jubilant on the mornings when

I woke up to dry blankets, but those were too few and far in-between. The night became a thing that frightened me, and it birthed the fear of not being in control.

As a result of these anxieties, I experienced horrible nightmares. Each night I dreamt of people chasing me and trying to kill me. If not that, it was big snakes trying to swallow me.

The night terrified me; fear never stopped, and the nightmares were constant. I was afraid of sleeping. Most times I would stay awake for as long as I could. The actual idea was to avoid sleep at all costs, but it never worked. I was beaten to a pulp and sworn at for wetting my bed.

In addition, the walk of shame to hang my blankets every morning was unbearable. Sometimes I would not hang my blankets, pretending they were not wet, just so that I would be spared from the walk of shame. This of course meant that I then would have to contend with sleeping on wet blankets and if caught, the beating would be even more severe and cruel.

It felt like I was the joke of '36' and that everyone in my community knew that I wet my blankets. My family thought if everyone knew, I would somehow be shamed into stopping.

I was not allowed to go on long trips. School was

unbearable as I was the kid with "soiled" and urine-smelling underwear. I hated those class-inspection days. I was the kid that everyone looked at, pointed fingers at and sometimes laughed at. It's funny, in retrospect that no one ever thought of looking into my background or for that matter why no one asked why another child who shared my address and surname passed all the cleanliness inspection and yet I failed.

I don't know when bed wetting stopped, but it was before I graduated from primary school. But by then the scars were already too deep, wide and rough. I had become a shell of myself. I had learnt to numb my feelings. I taught myself not to care who said what. I was so ashamed and so self-conscious I could not climb outside of myself. I withdrew into myself. I suspect this is where I took up introversion. I kept to myself as the effort of closing my ears to the despicable comments and stares was a bit much.

It was in dealing with shame when I discovered that the walls, I had built to protect myself were invisible, not just to the world but to myself as well. As a result, no matter how much I determined not to walk in shame, it still plagued me. I believe it took God to show me those hidden areas. For me to find a solution, I had to go back to those areas which cemented the notion of shame in my life. I started with the shame that came into my life when I was four years old got molested. I began to deal with subconscious conclusions, I had made about myself and life.

I thought it was my fault that I was molested. I concluded that I must have brought it upon myself, and that I did not deserve to be protected. I thought I was molested because I was ugly, and no one loves an ugly child. Don't ask me how I came to believe these lies, but I did. Moreover, I had to confront the view that said in order to protect myself I needed to be invisible and to shy away from attention.

One by one I went to those incidents that were a justification for shame to have power over my life. Once these thoughts were corrected, I began to live the truth of a shame-free life. Perhaps I am oversimplifying this process, but it was not simple. As it was not something I could have done on my own.

I needed the Holy Spirit to show me these experiences that cemented the power of shame in my life. I had to go to the thoughts I formulated during those experiences, and begin to break and remove them, by negating and replacing them with truth. I used the bible as my reference. I went back to who God created me to be and used His word to build the dominant thoughts that would control my life.

I truly underestimated how much shame had contributed to my need to be invisible. But I dealt with it, I suddenly had the need to be seen and to actually connect with people. Although I now live a shame-free life, I am sometimes tempted to withdraw into myself or to deflect attention, as I don't always know how to receive or enjoy attention in a healthy way.

However, I am learning to accept healthy attention and to embrace it as part of life. I learn mostly by observing how others treat the attention given to them. If you like, this is a process of allowing the child within to catch up with the adult self.

I was surprised in 2017 when someone I had been with to about three conferences or so, asked me where I had been all along. I was shocked at how my need to be invisible or be part of the background had worked so well. This showed me the power of brokenness. Brokenness was able to make someone as tall as me, with a loud voice and a bold laugh to be invisible, which is pretty remarkable. I know I am healed as these days it is hard for people to miss my presence even when I am silent. I carry a mantle of power and authority. I walk with confidence as I have overcome the worst of me and have embraced my true identity.

CHAPTER 8

The mask of confidence

I have always been known as a confident person and in fact, in some places people have said I am overconfident and 'cocky'. I had gladly accepted these labels, except that it was a lie. My display of confidence was nothing but that, a great charade.

An online dictionary defines confidence as the state of feeling certain about the truth of something and as a feeling of self-assurance arising from one's appreciation of one's own abilities or qualities.

Sure, in all my career life and some areas of my personal life, I had a degree of confidence. I also developed an arrogant persona to help me in those moments when I needed it. It did help that I had a great work ethic, intelligence, curiosity and an insatiable need to learn. This pretty much ensured that I enjoyed promotion everywhere I went, but it did not get rid of my lack of confidence.

Although this was a hidden struggle, I am certain that those who were able to look beyond the façade, came across the 'insecure and inadequate' woman I was. I had zero confidence. I felt like a fake. I hid myself, in the process, lost myself, and could not recall who I was before all the personalities I created became dominant.

Because of this, I developed an inconsistent personality that did not make sense. I would move from being overly confident to being a nervous wreck the next minute, without explanation. I had a multi personality disorder of sorts.

I could not understand how I did presentations in front of audiences all the time at work and yet could not stand on a stage and preach to people without falling apart. Or how I could easily hold conversations with great people in one area and then become tongue tied in another area.

Regardless of how well I did or how many accolades I received; I always underplayed my success. This helped me not to focus on how fake success made me feel. As a rule, I redirected any attention that I received. This was not intentional but had become an established behaviour.

It is funny though that I only discovered that I had 'confidence issues' three or four years ago when I was working through issues that hid this truth from me. Issues such as false humility, which I used to avert attention and arrogance that I masked with humour.

I did not believe in my worth, therefore no matter how well I did, I still could not overcome the deep-seated feelings of unworthiness. My intelligence often worked against me rather than for me. While I could accept people's complements about my intelligence, I could never celebrate it. It was not up to the standard of intelligence I had set for myself. In that way, I was never intelligent enough.

It did not help that I did not feel I could trust my mind. As in my late twenties, I became so forgetful that I thought there was something wrong with my mind. I could not retain any information at all. If by some luck I was able to retain some information, I would remember it sparsely. I would completely forget people I just met and the conversations I just had. I found that there were gaps in my memory, for instance certain periods or years of my life went missing from my memory.

One of the things that eventually got me to the doctor, was being in a job interview and not remembering whether I did project management or not. Yet when asked the principles of project management I could easily answer them. Furthermore, I passed a project management test given to me. There was a vague remembrance of going to a project management class, but I could not say for sure.

Forgetting altered my life so much that I learnt to write copious notes of everything. I also found a mechanism of dealing with people who expected me to know them and yet I had no memory of them. Thus, I learnt to overcome information retention problems.

The doctors could not find anything medically wrong with me even after a lot of scans and tests. When I got saved and my life changed, my ability to retain information improved somewhat. However, I only received complete healing during the Reconciliation Ministries International Conference held at Gateway Church International in 2016.

I attended Presbytery and in the process of receiving a word of prophecy, Pastor Barbara Garlington mentioned my inability to retain information. The team prayed for me and mentioned the toxins that have been hampering the functionality of my brain. This reminded me of the word of prophesy I had received about the need for the 'dross and the tin' to be removed out of me. I saw the faithfulness of God.

I received complete healing on that day and the inability to retain information, ended instantly. Not only did God heal my inability to retain information but my brain's functionality was also restored. My ability to think and comprehend things, became something of a marvel.

I still write many things down as it has become a habit. But I no longer take copious notes. What is amazing for me is realising that I don't always have to refer to my notes to remember stuff. I literally have to learn to be comfortable speaking without notes. In the past, I could never have attempted such. I am amazed at the levels my brain can go to. I can trust it to do what it was meant to do, without disappointing me.

The healing of my brain boosted my confidence. Even so, I only became completely confident after I had dealt with the source of why I felt unworthy and inadequate.

After I had dealt with my confidence issues, I had to deal with some of the unintended consequences of the lack of confidence, such as the need for approval and affirmation. If I didn't get affirmation after presenting or public speaking, I would doubt my delivery. I would overthink people's responses which

I would then use to determine whether or not I spoke well.

This may seem like the responsible thing to do, but it was a death trap. I was always interrogating my actions and conversations resulting in second guessing myself. Yep, my life was tiring. There was no time for rest.

In dealing with all of these issues, I also had to confront the lie I told myself, that I was an introvert. I was stunned to discover that my introversion was a result of the trauma and not something I was born with.

Introverts live in their heads and are energised by time spent alone. Most introverts are prone to over analysing and over thinking. Therefore, what added to my challenge of public speaking was that while speaking I would also be analysing the audience and the impact of what I was saying.

Sometimes I would be so lost in overthinking that I would lose track of what I was saying in the first place. As a result, I could not connect with my audience. Other times I would get myself so overwhelmed while talking that I would cut my speech short.

Many times, the speech in my mind would sound different to the one I was delivering, and I would fail to reconcile the two. This also played itself out in individual conversations where I would have an entire conversation with the next person in my mind without having an actual conversation with that person.

Often people would classify my failure at public speaking as a lack of confidence or to being nervous, but it was mostly an issue of over-thinking. I know this because when I am truly nervous, I tremble and struggle to breathe or hold a thought. The funny thing though, was that public speaking in my professional spaces was somehow not so much of a problem. Perhaps it was because it mainly required head knowledge rather than heart engagement.

Introverted people often find life in their minds more interesting than actual things and most people. This makes it difficult for them to break free of their mental reality. I personally struggled with staying present and I would day-dream habitually. This is why I needed the help of the Holy Spirit to help me stay present. I was always recording conversations and experiences for later use instead of actually being in those moments. I was not in touch with my emotions and would often realise I was hurting or unhappy long after the fact.

Therapy helped me uncover and deal with these

issues. After I had dealt with them, I learned that I needed to redefine the meaning of true confidence and to start walking in it. The key for me was in learning that true confidence, is not a 'one-two-three step' type of thing, it had to come from within. My confidence now comes from embracing who God made me to be and who God is to me. It was amazing to understand that the abilities I was created with, are not dependent on what people think of me or what I think of myself, but on who I was made to be. This is particularly significant for me because I can set unreasonable expectations for myself. It's freeing to accept that I am human, and that *while I may pursue excellence, perfection is not required.*

I also had to learn not to live for human approval but to embrace God's approval. God's approval has nothing to do with what I do or don't do, but everything to do with who He is. Now I do well as an extension of who I am not because I am seeking to please or be approved of. This has brought freedom to my life.

I also had to learn to be confident, without being arrogant and underplaying my achievements. I am now convinced that God has bestowed great intelligence upon me.

It is incredible what my mind is able to do without

much effort. I can succeed in every subject I focus on and without much effort. This is an incredible gift that I cannot take credit for, it's a testament of the greatness of God.

I am conscious that sometimes, while learning new habits and new responses, old ways can creep in. This has taught me to be intentional and aware of my reactions. I am reliant on God and those around me to keep me accountable in my journey of healing, especially because sometimes, there is a thin line between bad and good habits. For instance, as someone who fancies herself a fiction writer, I love observing people, and I am always recording conversations and mannerisms, for character development.

However, while this is fun, I have to do it without substituting making real conversations with the ones in my mind. Crazy right? Well, as they say, "the struggle is real".

Even so, I have a new lease on life. I appreciate what it means to be unbound, like someone who was in jail. I no longer have to hide my creativity and self-expression. I have made a commitment to be true to myself and to live boldly for Jesus. I have not let go of the principles that guide my life but I have changed the approach.

In gaining my freedom, I am learning to allow

those around me the freedom to be and to avoid imposing myself on them. Thoughtfulness does not come by magically; it has to be developed and I am cultivating that culture in my life.

CHAPTER 9

Letting go of control, learning dependence and embracing vulnerability!

Until a light is cast, what was in the dark remains invisible to the naked eye. Yet what is invisible has an ability to control your actions, whether you are aware of it if or not. Such was the power of "the need to be in control" in my life.

Where I came from, the denial of food was used as a form of punishment, so I taught myself not to need food. I determined that if I did not have to eat, food would not be used against me. Similarly, whenever I needed money for something at school, it came with conditions. This is how I got to hate depending on others for money.

There were many other things used as a means of control, but these two things, food and money, were the biggest motivation for my need to be in control of my life and not be dependent on anyone. I learnt from an early age that each time I depended on anyone I always ended up being hurt or disappointed.

I learned that I was the only person I could confidently rely on. As flawed as that concept was, it became my truth. It made me obsess with control. I had a need to control everything, conversations, relationships and projects etc. If I was not in control, I was uncomfortable, defensive and easily scared. Just as I did not want to depend on anyone, anyone that depended on me was an unwanted burden. I sought to make myself emotionally unavailable.

Every single experience in life has an upside and a downside. The positive thing about being obsessed with control is that it made me successful in my career. I always successfully implemented projects, regardless of the size, time constraints and complexity. I was in control of every single step, even what I had delegated. I thoroughly thought through every step, potential risks and solutions, such that there was no room for failure. This resulted in a lot of applause for me each time.

The downside was that I was always given more work than I could carry, which meant constant burn-out. I struggled with perfection, which meant delegation was an impossible ask. I micro-managed and stifled those I had delegated tasks to. Sometimes I would succeed in controlling my need for perfection, but sometimes I would not. This meant that I was never satisfied with my performance or of those I managed.

I had a need for things to be packed or placed in a certain way. CDs, books, plates and everything else had to be arranged in a particular way that only made sense to me. I spent a lot time reorganising my house after my helper had gone home for the day.

The times when I lived with people, I would sometimes lash out on them for things that were not arranged in a particular way. I was impossible to live with. I developed tendencies of someone who suffered from an Obsessive-Compulsive Disorder (OCD).

The need to control deterred me from real connection with people. Unless I was in control, I could not connect. It did not help that I could not depend on people, as I subconsciously did not trust them. There was always fear that they might hurt me and as a result I would lose them. I guess I never saw forgiveness as part of the equation. I also did not like people depending on me as I was afraid that I might let them down and possibly scar them, the way I was scarred.

There were those whose dependency aroused resentment in me, especially when I thought it clingy. I felt suffocated. I had one particular friend who once told me she did not want to be friends with me anymore, as I was not *emotionally available*. At the time, I thought she was being difficult. In retrospect, she probably was the only person who refused to accept my brokenness as normal.

It took a disaster that landed me in a financial crisis, to accept help from friends. However, throughout their intervention I still had a need to pay careful attention, as I felt they may use their assistance to gain control over me. Indeed, it took a while to see that they did not expect any inappropriate thing from me. Conversations about my finances made me uncomfortable and defensive. My reaction to their offer for help somehow prompted me to question why I was afraid of being helped.

I suspect my friends were no wiser with the battle that ensued within me. As I had an 'alter ego' that was alright with asking for help and being open, especially as I was always willing to help. My friends did not think they were doing anything that I would not do. Except that whereas I was quick to help, I hated getting help. Somehow, I thought it good to help others but I could not trust others to help me.

My need to control was steeped in my inability to trust people's intentions. I still remember that learning to trust my therapist was a scary thing. I remember the first time she asked me to let go of my need to control my reactions, I literally had heart palpitations because of anxiety. She had to reassure me repeatedly that she was not going to hurt me. Even though my mind knew this, I still had to do breathing exercises to help me calm down. It took a while to let go of controlling my reactions to her questions, especially the ones that touched unhealed scars.

Once I had dealt with 'not being in control', *dependency and vulnerability* were sorted. However, I still had to change my perspective which was framed by hurt, violation and abuse.

Now I know that *life is not about being in control of every situation and person, but about being in rhythm, with the song of life.* It is about understanding that, although the song may be sad and painful, you do not stop singing because that's what enhances the beautiful parts.

I made a commitment to allow myself to depend on others and deal with whatever discomfort came with it. A one-step-at-a-time process, which gets easier with practice. I am sure it will eventually be a normal thing for me. Likewise, with vulnerability I had to make it a necessary part of life.

I had to practice teaching myself not to hide or run from situations that made me vulnerable. This included visiting places that, made me feel emotionally exposed or vulnerable, as I could not hide myself or be in control. I was not aware that God had worked in me to bring me to a complete place of healing until a few months later. I had a work trip to Eastern Cape and told Moruti Matshepo about it.

The Sunday before I left, she gave me R50 and told me "ke ya mofao" (pocket money). I was very pleased, and grateful, primarily as no one had ever done that for me. I went to Eastern Cape and came back without having touched the R50 because I was so excited about it. I kept opening my wallet to look at it, that money became the most valuable thing I owned.

As time passed something started happening. Every time I looked at the R50 or thought of it, I was filled with child-like excitement. Just thinking about what I would buy, brought back child-like glee. I was back at being a child and it felt like I had hit a jackpot and my delight was palpable.

I have always liked money but during my childhood, it was used as a source of power and control that distorted my view of money. Although I had been working since high school I did not value money and neither held it in high esteem. It was not anything to be respected, but a tool for inflicting pain and control.

Those who hurt me used resources to express the extent of their control. Therefore, I succeeded so that I would never have to depend on anyone for money or any other thing. Having money meant I would always be in control.

Consequently, I was uncomfortable with being given money, as I always wondered what that person wanted in return. Unless I had worked for the money, I was uncomfortable with being given money. Moruti Matshepo is someone I trust; someone I know has my best interests at heart and would never intentionally hurt me. So, when she gave me money, something in me that was destroyed in my childhood, was restored. The simple act of giving me what I did not need, something that expressed her love and care, showed me the beauty of God's generosity.

In this experience money ceased to be an instrument of pain or a possible tool of abuse. God used this experience to restore what was taken away during my childhood. I am grateful to Moruti Matshepo for her generosity and her heart. I am not sure if that money would have achieved what God wanted it to do in my life, had it come from someone else.

Each day I am learning that letting go of control, requires being intentional, teaching yourself to trust and to continually say yes to trusting in order to maintain your gain. You need to do this even when there is a possibility of being hurt. Fully trusting that God has the ability to protect and heal us from such.

For me learning to trust is like building a house. I needed to ensure that my foundation is surefooted first by trusting God. Then I needed to receive the assurance that I am safe in His hands. Being fully aware of who God is in my life, and who He has made me to be, keeps my hope alive. This way, trusting people becomes an extension of who I am rather than a function I perform. This gives me comfort that should the walls or the roof of my house collapse, I would be able to rebuild because the foundation is intact.

'Not trusting' was my default position for all my life. Therefore, in renewing my mind I needed to cement the truth that trusting is my default standing unless there is a reason not to trust. I did this until trusting was established as my natural reaction to things.

Therefore, when something confronts my decision to trust, I stand against that thought and remind myself of the truth, trusting is my natural habitat.

I suspect promotion and greater responsibility allowed me to relinquish control in my professional life, before I even knew that control was such a stronghold for me. I realised, at work that in order for people to learn they had to be given room to find themselves and to make mistakes and this is impossible under micromanagement.

I also learned that work becomes a better place if you allow people to be themselves, while you commit to serving them by helping them improve what they bring to the table. You will have a team that is empowered, happy and excited to achieve the set goals. This has characterised my leadership style. As a result, I have successfully mentored and empowered a lot of people.

I love empowering people; it gives me great joy to see them excelling and achieving what they were created to do. My success is a team's success and does not lead to ill health and overthinking every part of the process. I have become a better teacher, coach and leader because of my experiences.

I have made it my goal to open myself to life and its experiences. I am working to allow myself to be more vulnerable and to experience life as it happens. I teach myself, every day, to bring all of me into every situation. Indeed, this is not easy, but I do my best. I carefully monitor my body language as it is easy for my body language to subconsciously aid me with dis-engaging from life. Take a simple thing such as folding hands. While I sometimes fold my hands when I don't know what to do with them, sometimes I fold them because I am uncomfortable.

CHAPTER 10

Getting over the hurdles

It is always the difficult, the impossible and the worst of horrors that call us to a higher ground. In the beginning of therapy as layers peeled off, I was uncomfortable with the person being unearthed. She was a stranger and the excitement of getting to know her was declining. The change was too rapid. It seemed like just as I was beginning to form an opinion about who I was, there would be another change that would catch me by surprise.

A case in point, I had lived all my life, self-identifying as an introvert, only to realise that I was more accurately both an introvert and an extrovert.

This fact alone irritated me so much, as it meant I had to unpack what all this meant. Discovering that you are not something that you thought you were, does not help you get rid of doing things that you used to do. This is very frustrating, as it requires you to redefine things. I was at odds with myself.

It was a strange feeling as I truly was meeting myself for the first time. I suspect that if it was not for therapy I would have given up. I learned to open myself to the process in spite of the discomfort. I had to make a decision to enjoy the journey of self-discovery; to embrace the surprises and the seemingly irrational moments.

What was even more difficult was not knowing how to respond to my family. While I was no longer angry with them, I was not sure of how I felt about them. When I asked my therapist about this, she advised me to give it time and allow my heart to speak for itself when it is ready. Well, she did not say this, in these specific words, this is what I deduced.

Sometimes my mind would get in my way, as I would wonder if my heart would ever get there, further I wondered how I would know when I got there.

During this time, I withdrew from active ministry and I suspect I would have stopped working if I could afford it. The responsibility of dealing with myself became burdensome. I only wanted to do what I had to do and nothing more. I created a bit of space between my cousins and I. They were a strong reminder of the uncomfortable truth I was still needing to digest. I needed time to come to terms with the fact that our re-collection of our childhood were opposite poles.

Much of what happened to me, was done in secret. It was done so expertly that if anyone happened to pay any attention, they would have discovered a beautiful picture of a loving and doting family. While in the past it was enough to remember positive childhood memories, the truth that these happened at the cost of my abuse was unbearable. Some of the beautiful memories now represented my complicity in the abuse. I lied, protected and did not expose the activities behind closed doors. Therefore no one came to save me.

I am aware that forgetting what happened to me was a coping mechanism. It was a way of dealing with what I was incapable of handling, emotionally. In spite of all that, I still needed to deal with how it betrayed me. I could not hold it against my cousins for having had a better life while I had suffered.

I love my cousins, but somehow being in their presence reminded me of 'the elephant in the room'. I was not ready to deal with my aunts and the history that had crept into my presence. I did not know what to do with all the strong emotions I suddenly felt.

There were so many things that I could not reconcile. How did I convince myself that my childhood was happy for all these years? How did I believe the lie I sold to myself for so long? When I realized the extent of the pain my family caused me in my childhood it was unbearable.

The pain that had caused me to create this perfect world that was a lie, said to me that I did not want them in my life; which in a sense, was madness as I am family-centric. Therefore, these thoughts were enough to build a lot of pointless frustration and anger. The resurrection of pain previously hidden was one of the most difficult experiences I have ever had.

When the current picture collides with history, it leaves you dumb-founded. How do you deal with the fact that the people you held in high regard, hurt you so much that you suppressed that experience? I wanted to run away from myself but could not.

I wanted to take my heart, set it aside and only take it back once it was healed, but this was not possible either. I slowly and reluctantly conceded defeat. I began to deal with my painful emotions. I engaged with them, questioned where they came from, what caused them and what made them so painful? I began to trace them to their roots and dealt with them at their source. I moved from being angry to being numb and at other times all I did was cry. I bombard myself and God with a rivulet of questions.

After weeks of crying and working through difficult memories, it was clear that I did not hate my aunts. I was shocked and hurt by the realisation that they had a part in my pain. Even so, I still loved them and was able to separate them from their actions. The desire to re-connect with them, re-surfaced. Please don't mistake that desire with a need to forget and embrace all, it was a need to explore how my heart would respond to them.

At this time my therapist advised me to mentally establish the type of relationship I wanted with my family. To set the parameters of our engagement. I am yet to fully do this, but I have taken the first step. I have to rewire my brain to respond differently to how I used to respond, as I had set a 'defence mechanism' that I was not aware of. Sometimes I find my-old-self responding and I somehow need to remind myself, nope I am no longer that person, I no longer need you to help me overcome. I am a healed and I am a different person.

I am learning how to connect with people without setting defensive boundaries, knowing fully-well that embracing vulnerability is not always going to be easy, but it's necessary for a fulfilling life. I made a commitment to be genuine in my connection with people. This means being true to my emotions and not forcing myself to do something because it is a must but doing it because it is good.

CHAPTER 11

Getting rid of the skunk!

The hardest thing about being misused is the impact, especially as the impact is not always obvious to you. For instance, I have always wondered why when my love language is touch, I didn't like being touched most times. It's like that little feeling that nudges at you, but you can't make sense of it.

Try as I may, I could never figure this out until recently. I remember my paternal grandmother's funeral a few years back, this was just after being saved. This was the first time I had gone back to my paternal grandmother's house in Lesotho, since my mother had stolen me from my grandparents.

It was a surreal experience. It was the first time I saw where my father was buried and had a chance to meet my father's family as an adult. After we exchanged pleasantries, this particular uncle attempted to kiss me, as was tradition in my father's family. I objected as I felt repulsed deep in my heart. I literally felt the anger rise, when I remembered how he violated me, when I was a five-year-old. I could not believe that he had the audacity to think I would welcome his perverted need to be friendly. I managed to push him off and ignored him the entire day without raising eyebrows, which would have left me with having to answer questions I was not ready to.

I pushed this experience aside after the funeral. Unfortunately, what I did not realise was that I still needed to deal with its impact. My uncle was like a father to me. After my father died, I was left at my paternal grandmother's house and I looked up to him. He gave me attention; protected me and even played with me. So, when he violated me, every bone of trust in me was shattered, not just towards him, but towards every man who was to come into my life. I closed myself off from most men. It seems I made a conclusion that men who say they love you, violate you. My uncle had threatened me into silence, which birthed isolation and fear.

The questions that bothered me even as an adult, was how come no one saw anything? How come no one noticed the sudden shame I had with my body? How come no one protected me? Why was I left alone with this predator? I could not get answers to these questions and the more I wondered the angrier I got.

For the longest time I was angry, because I could not fathom how someone would bathe me and not discover that something was wrong. Surely there were signs that could have been seen. This caused me prolonged angst, as I could never look at my family and not get angry.

In retrospect, it is perhaps why I was uprooted from my paternal Grandma's house to live with my aunt. I am however still at a loss as to why no one thought to return me to my mother at that stage or to deal with my uncle in a manner that ensured he never touched me again.

While my aunt's house was a safe haven from sexual molestation, it had its own challenges. My aunt thought I was old enough to cook, mind you I was about six at the time. I remember quite clearly how I learned to place the Prima Stove on the floor, switch it on and cook. It was this very thing that gave my mother an idea to steal me away from my paternal grandparents.

My mom was livid, when she one day came to visit and found me cooking. She kept saying "they have turned you into a woman". I did not understand what the big deal was, as I was proud that I could cook.

I forgot so many things, including this experience. When I hit my 20s, I found myself hating the idea of cooking. It felt like slavery and I did everything in my power to avoid it. Little did I know that I was fighting for the child who was forced to cook at age 6. I had also forgotten that I was raped when I was nine. I buried the knowledge until it was triggered at a funeral in 2016. I felt betrayed by the adults in my life yet again and by my own mind.

Again, I went through a series of questions I have had when these kinds of memories came tumbling down. The scars were deep and multi-layered. I had built a myriad of invisible walls around me, in an attempt to protect myself. I hated myself, I hated my body and worked hard at self-destructing.

My family broke my spirit, through molestation, physical and verbal abuse. As I walk through healing, I wonder how I managed to survive at all. This is because when I look back into my past, I see that there was nothing but a flimsy thread holding my life together.

If it were not for God the thread that held me together would have be torn apart, but somehow

God used it to sustain me. This is testament of God's goodness. I don't know, how else one would explain how I managed to live through the trauma that I went through, except to say by the grace of God.

It does not matter how brave and confident I appeared to be. The truth is I always wore masks to survive. I feared life. I was petrified of being myself. I was frightened to love or be loved. While I complained that no one knew me, I did not know myself. I ensured that no one came close enough to know me. I was constantly changing and adapting to new circumstances. At the end, I adopted characteristics and behaviours of other people. I lost myself in the process.

I was once told to be myself, and that threw a curve ball in my court. This was primarily because I did not know what it meant to be me. I did not know who I was. The 'self' I knew was the one I had created. And the being I created was circumstance based.

One of the things that shocked me in therapy was to come face to face with the personalities I had created. I had a clear picture of my life. The real me was a scared child, who sat coiled in a corner, hidden in a heavily covered cocoon; encircled by branches of the different personalities. Some had existed for such a long time, I thought of them as my real identity.

I did not know who I was. This was also reflected

on how I dressed. I dressed like everyone around me. I had not realised this until my mentor commented about my clothes. When I realised the validity of her comments, I went through my wardrobe and I was shocked at what I found there.

I honestly felt like an alien had taken over my wardrobe. I had one particular dress that made me look like a pregnant woman. It also made sense why I couldn't change the colour of my house from the standard white walls for the longest time. The idea of painting my house into any colour felt like getting naked in the middle of a busy street. A scary thought.

I think my ability to bring together people from diverse cultures and backgrounds, was possibly because my multiple personalities mirrored their diversity. It was because of this that I pulled back from people. While going through the process of healing, I needed space to find out who I was in absence of external influence.

I also had to acknowledge that I had struggled to commit to relationships. This brought another uncomfortable truth home. Like I briefly mentioned in chapter six. I was not sure if I had ever fallen in love. I am talking about that kind of crazy, undiluted and unadulterated kind of love.

Although I had a few relationships in the past, I

have always been in control. There were parts of me that I never opened up. I was always guarded. If there was a possibility of ever falling in-love, I found a way of sabotaging the relationship or running away.

Part of my healing meant false branches had to be severed. Other people get to this place by peeling the layers but in my case, it was cutting the branches and breaking off the thick glass walls that surrounded me. Getting myself freed was difficult. It meant letting go of the personalities I had adopted and things that had been identified as part of me.

I was advised not to place unfair expectations on myself, to avoid self-judgement and to be patient. This helped because to not know yourself can be disconcerting. Yes, you would probably still like the same food and movies, but your response to things changes. Sometimes I sounded like someone I did not like, and my default response was shutting that person down, until I remembered the counsel I had received.

Over time I learnt to accept myself and got to know the new me. I discovered living life from within. It was a revelation that living your life according to the circumstances you find yourself in, is detrimental.

I needed to replace old perverted principles with new Godly ones. For instance, in learning to redefine what love meant for me, I took my definition of love from God Almighty, who is love.

First, I had to accept His love for me and embrace it. After accepting Gods love, I learnt that it was only through loving myself that I could truly love others. I had to accept who I was created to be with all the scars. I also had to accept that while I would have preferred a different experience, my horrible past contributed to who I had become. I had to open myself to God's restoration.

For the first time, loving others as I loved myself became a reality. Abuse can make you hate yourself while you love others. Somewhere in your psyche you believe that you are not worthy of love, yet others are. Part of my healing was to forgive myself for the part I played in destroying myself and to accept myself as I was before I could move toward who I would like to be. Doing this brought me to a place where I could learn to love myself.

Loving myself freed me to love people the way God wants me to. I discovered that when you love people out of who you are, it does not matter whether or not they love you back. As love is an expression of yourself, rather than an action you are taking towards the next person.

Indeed, the love, you have for the next person would dictate certain actions to express that love but loving them transcends your expression of that love. Your expression of love is what enables the next person to reciprocate or receive your love.

After discovering myself, I went through my wardrobe and got rid of clothes that didn't reflect me. This was probably the hardest thing I had to do but also sometimes the funniest. My clothes were a true reflection of my 'multiple personalities' era. Going through each item to assess whether or not it was me, was initially daunting. For a while I was lethargic and depressed to undertake it.

I eventually decided to let go of the task and pray about it. I prayed particularly for God to help me see clearly, to help me resolve the conflict in my heart. I also needed him to help me understand why I struggled to let go of the clothes that were not me. I found out that getting rid of them was putting an end to the false personalities I had created. This felt like I was killing parts of me.

This realisation strengthened my resolve to let go of the clothes that were not me. Doing this was like giving permission to the new me to find space to express herself and define who she is.

If you knew me for a year and meet me today, the difference is distinct and significant. I am having fun and I enjoy taking myself out for shopping. I am like a child who discovered her favourite candy store and has a "blank cheque" to buy as much candy as she wants.

CHAPTER 12

I wish I had known him

What is a father and what does a relationship with a father look like? I had not thought about this question until now. My father died when I was four, but I have always had strong men who played that role in my life. Indeed, the few men that violated me, broke me, but the many that built me really played their part.

I never quite felt the loss of my father, as I was too young when he died. I think things changed when the men who had an impact in my life died too. I lost so many people to death, that I eventually stopped crying. In refusing to cry I was taking my power from death, at least I thought so.

I did not know that my tears would dry up in all areas. I would become sad but would not be able to express that sadness. This hardened my heart and denied me the opportunity to deal with pain. Not being able to cry was good for a while, but eventually it started to kill me. I got used to numbing my feelings.

I had created an unnecessary challenge for myself, which further complicated my life. It was only after I got born again that the ability to cry was restored. But the need to cry for my father never came up. I cried that I had lost my mother, but I did not cry for losing my father.

In 2017 I discovered that *learning to live with a disability does not make you unaffected by it, it merely means you learn to live with its limitations*. It turned out that I had learned to overcome life without a father, but I had not dealt with what it meant to not have a father.

When this truth hit me, I became aware of how confident girls who have good fathers are. I saw how easily they relate with men. This observation made me realise that in spite of having had strong male figures, because of the few men who violated me, men in general had become objects of my fear. While I could confidently deal with men on an intellectual level, I could not deal with them on an emotional level.

This is why at the height of my self-destruction;

men became objects to play with. In those days, I could only be in a relationship if I was in control or emotionally unavailable. Things changed after I got saved, but the deep-rooted fear of men did not.

I found myself exposed to genuinely good men, who loved their families and their wives, but I could not cope with this picture. I would watch from a distance to see if they were pretending to be good or not. When it became apparent that they were genuine people, I would relax a bit, but I could not let my guard completely down.

I can't recall what made me realise I had an irrational fear of men. But it was something I needed to deal with and overcome. Doing this brought me to a painful realisation that I was sad to have lost my father. I did not have the opportunity to know him. I grieved for him, like he had just died.

I had to get to a place of being acquiescent that my father was dead. I had to let go of wondering if things that I experienced would have happened had he been alive. I replayed the tapes of my life and imagined every scene with my father in it. This only served to bring the truth home, I had no father and he was not coming back.

Eventually I came to a place of acceptance. For the first time in my life I cried that my father was not there and that he had not been there all my life. I cried that he would never give me counsel about men and particularly that he would never walk me down the aisle.

The thought that my father would not give me away to my husband was the hardest part; especially because my younger brother, whom I had always thought would do the onus, died unexpectedly. I had always thought I would die before him, as the first born of the family. The fact that I was the sole survivor of my nucleus family was devastating.

I entertained so many regrets about the life decisions that I had taken for a while. I thought that, perhaps if I had married at 23 when I received my first marriage proposal, I would at least have a family of my own to comfort me. I knew though that, I might have perpetuated the brokenness I had and that my marriage might have ended in divorce.

All my life, I was convinced that one day my brother would get married and have children. Therefore, I never felt the need to have children and in fact did not want to, for many years. I was afraid that I would inflict the atrocities perpetrated against me, onto them. I was afraid that my kids would be as broken as I was.

I thought that just like I hated my family my

children would have hated me. This was a good enough deterrence. The fact that when I die my family line would possibly die with me was a hard one. I don't know how I got through this period. I guess the discipline of therapy teaches you to deal with things as they come. Even though dealing with them, at times means praying for yourself and working through difficult questions. You do this because you know that eventually you will be victorious.

I conquered when I accepted that I had no say in losing my father, mother and brother. I had to realise that no matter how I willed and wished it they were never going to come back. I had to accede to the life decisions I had made, let go of regret and be content with my current life as is.

I also had to acknowledge that when I get married, I might not be able to have kids even though I want them, and I had to be fine with that. I do not regulate the future, but I control how I live today. The best I can do is live well and enjoy every moment of my life.

The process of relating to men on an emotional basis continues slowly. I guess the difficulty is that the threat of violence against women in South Africa is real. Which makes it difficult to level the playing-field and not paint everyone with the same brush.

BUT I have hope.

My current environment is filled with good men. I am learning to open up around men and each day I remind myself that not all men are violent and not all men desire to hurt me. I am beginning to relax around men and to allow myself the joy of their company.

CHAPTER 13

Veni vidi vici

To be honest, I was not going to write this chapter. Precisely as the subject of my brother has been a sore area for the longest of times. My brother came into the world in 1977 on the 18th of January, 1 year 9 months and ten days after I was born. He was named Lebusa (the one who rules) Joseph Noko. Aptly named as from a very young age, he commanded loyal followers.

My brother and I were separated when I was six years old and he was just about to turn four. The next time I saw him again, I was eleven and it was at our mother's funeral. I kept thinking; how horrible my mother's passing must have been for him. I was at a loss, but I could not justify my pain. I thought his pain was more valid than mine. After my mother's funeral I next saw my brother when I was seventeen years old doing grade eleven. He just showed up, one night without warning.

It seems he had paid attention to all the times when my maternal grandmother would ask him to come visit. He arrived in a taxi from Lesotho with a small bag of clothes. My grandmother swiftly arranged for the taxi driver to be paid and did not waste any time taking him to a sangoma so that he could be cleansed from "senyama" (bad omen), as they put it. She also quickly reported his matter to the police station, primarily as she was scared that my father's family might come knocking.

His identity documents were arranged. He was in high school when he left Lesotho. However, since he had no proof of school attendance and could not speak or write Afrikaans, he was demoted to grade five in primary school. This was the mercy granted to him so that he could learn Afrikaans.

I can't say we were any close then as the gap between us was too wide. Plus, my family was behaving un-characteristically. While food used to be hidden from or be used as a form of punishment against me, he was treated like a prince. We were pretty much not allowed to shout at him, even when he was wrong. It was as if his pain was greater than mine, at least that's how my family made me feel. My grandmother was out to heal my brother's wound of having our mother die without him knowing her.

Home was stressful to me, so when I was twenty, I moved out. I got an apartment in Yeoville, which I shared with a colleague. When it was time for her to move back to Belgium, I moved back to Soweto. I rented myself a backroom until a few years later when I could afford to move back to Yeoville. At least this time around I could afford my own apartment. I started helping out my grandmother financially and would once in a while buy clothes for my brother.

I guess we started to have a better relationship when one day, after visiting for Christmas, he decided he was not going back to my grandmother's house in Orlando East. He told me hair-raising stories of how he was treated. I was shocked at how bad things had become. It seems when I moved out of home, my family had a need to take out their madness onto him, as he was just the perfect person. This was the first real conversation we had, and it was the beginning of our relationship.

We found a school and enrolled him. He was the oldest grade 10 student as he was twenty-two at the time. In a matter of a few weeks, I became an instant mom. The struggle of balancing being both a sister and a mother was tough, especially as my brother was spoiled rotten. We fought about everything. He revolted when I wanted him to clean the house and cook. We also fought about curfew times and the amount of TV he could watch. Especially as I only started owning a TV set when he came to live with me.

It was tough. My family was angry that I took him to come live with me, but they did not express this anger directly to me. However, I would get calls from concerned relatives, who were conduits of expression for my family's disappointment. The only thing that got me through this, I suppose, was the fact that my family's opinion did not really matter at time.

Eventually we found a rhythm and got to a place of harmony. The challenge came when he failed Grade 11. His report said he was a slow learner. He wanted to wallow in pity, but I told him that was a lie, all he needed to do was to focus on his studies.

He resolved to do better the following year. However, the impact of living in a place like Yeoville and going to school where opulence was on his face, pressured him. Suddenly he wanted branded clothes and all sorts of things that I could not afford. I would like to think this is why he decided to start stealing, but I will never know. I found out about his criminal activities when he was jailed for being in possession of ammunition. I was so furious that I did not bail him until two days later.

When Siya and I went to bail him, his skin had broken out into some strange rash, that he could not stop scratching. It seems that was a good wakeup call, as he knew that he could not survive jail. The next two years went by swiftly and he graduated high school. He enrolled to do an IT course in one of those questionable colleges, but I was happy that he was at least studying.

The difficulty of our relationship was the fact that giving him the life he had, came at a great sacrifice to me. I could not pursue my own studies as I was paying for his. Although he complained about having only a few branded clothes, he dressed far better than I did. I could not afford the clothes I bought for him. Yet in spite of this, he did not appreciate the sacrifice I made for him. He soon dropped out from his IT course and was back to stealing. When I found out I gave him an ultimatum, stop stealing or move out. He decided to the latter.

I moved to Kensington and started afresh, I was angry at him and I resented that he squandered every opportunity I gave him. Above all I was angry that I had given up on my dreams for him. Two years later he came back and asked for forgiveness. He claimed to have stopped stealing, and like a fool I bought his lie. In the two years he was on his own, his friends had tried to kill him twice. First, they burned his backroom while he was sleeping inside and when that did not work, they tried poisoning him. I really believed he would cut ties with them, but that was just my imagination.

A friend of mine worked for Mr Price, so I asked her to organise a temp job for him. For a while things seemed to be working out. Back in those days I used to travel a lot. I remember the one trip I was on; I can't remember whether it was while I was in Germany or Sweden. I had been gone for two weeks and that was enough time for him to go back to stealing.

When I got back home, after unpacking, I went to his room to place his gift on his bed. Only to find a suitcase full of stolen items on the floor. Clothes still wrapped in the original packets, sunglasses and shoes. I knew that the stuff was stolen from a shop, because the price tags were still there.

When I searched his room, I found a gun and bullets, I threw these away. I was livid. How could he bring this stuff into my house, I wondered? How could he go back to stealing? I kept asking myself. I was in turmoil. He did not come back home for a few days. I called all his friends, and no one knew where he was.

Clearly, the police had been watching him as the night he came back home they were onto him. I was relieved that he was caught, as I was scared that he could get killed otherwise. I did not bail him or attend his court hearings.

I was furious with my family. When I called to inform them about what happened, they were more upset that I threw away his gun and not the fact that he was stealing. This is when I decided to write my family off. It was clear to me that they did not love my brother, because they liked the benefits of the criminal life he led; and did not worry that he was causing misery to other people.

My brother somehow managed to wiggle himself out of jail but he did not come back to my house. As he thought I had called the police on him.

I bought my first townhouse and moved to Sundowner; this was a few months after I had given my life to Christ. My life changed completely and because of what God had done for me, when my brother came crawling back, I was only happy to forgive him. Except that yet again after another long overseas trip I came back to an empty house.

The only hint I had that whatever happened to my brother was serious, was the soaked clothes in the bathtub which had started to rot. I looked for him everywhere and called every friend I knew. Only to discover that he was jailed in my absence. This time around I did not even want to know why. Unfortunately for him, the police had a serious case and they were unwilling to be bought. He was sentenced to 10 years.

The first three and half years, I did not visit or even think about him. I could not be bothered. I was furious with him and to a great degree I had hardened my heart towards him. Things changed when God started to convict me about my unwillingness to forgive him. For a while I reasoned with God. I argued that I had forgiven my brother, but I just did not want to see him. The futile argument went on and on for weeks until I admitted the truth. When I realised the depth of my anger and resentment towards him, I repented and asked for God to give me grace to forgive him.

Eventually I gathered enough strength to forgive him and visited him in jail. I brought a friend along as I was not sure if I could do it alone. We never did speak in depth, but I told him how I felt. He did what he usually did, apologised and promised to walk on the straight and narrow. He vowed that he had learned his lesson. I believed him and fell back into the big sister role of taking care of him.

My brother, the charming lanky lad who was handsome like my father, was a marvel. Although he was dark skinned like my father and was a mirror image of him, we looked alike somehow. I never believed it when we were growing up, as I had taken my mother's light skin tone and was a spitting image of hers. I thought the only thing I had in common with my brother, was the shape of our noses. I guess my nose is the one thing that I took after my father. My mother had what we called an English nose.

After six years my brother was released on parole. Since I could not yet trust him and back then I travelled frequently, we agreed that he would move in with my grandmother. He found a job, which after three months he complained about. He said he could hardly afford transport. I told him it was important for him to keep himself occupied with work, so I volunteered to subsidise his transport.

Little did I know that I opened up a door for him to try and be a saviour of the world. If he was not buying that or giving money to a certain relative, he was opening clothing accounts he could not afford. I realised the futility of trying to assist him and withdrew my help eventually.

When I did that, he started stealing at work to augment the shortfall he had. He was caught and summarily fired. When he told me, I laughed at him and asked him what he had expected. A bit cruel I know. I told him; he must be glad that they did not open a case against him. I was insensitive, but sometimes when you are confronted with a ridiculously painful and overwhelming situation, you laugh. *If you ever wondered why President Zuma laughed so much, now you know.*

This led to a spiral of things. In order to cope with life, he started going to the mashonisas[3]. I ended up having to intervene and pay his debts as they refused to give him mercy and took his identity document, which meant he could not look for work. Soon enough he was accused of stealing things and selling them. However, he claimed innocence and sold me a story of how much he was suffering.

I got him an outside room in Evaton, hoping that a change of scenery would do him good. I was trying to help this grown man, who should have been on his own, to get his life in order. Just so that he could stop depending on me.

That only worked for a few months. Soon he was

---

3 Money Lenders

back at 'complaining and unending pity' parties. This was a good reason for him to go back to stealing. When I heard this, I was furious and told him that I was going to call the police on him. He ran away from Evaton and moved back to my Grandmother's house. But when he heard that police were still looking for him, he ran.

For months, we did not know where he was. Until he showed up in my office, smelling like a dump. I was flabbergasted, I did not know how to respond. My brother who used to wear the most expensive perfume was living on the streets. Driving him to Orlando East, to my granny's house, I discovered that he, in fact, only came back home because he was sick. He smelled so bad; we could not close the car windows. It was such an awkward situation. While I was dealing with the pain of seeing him like that, I was worried about lice being left in my car. I felt like such a hypocrite. This in a way helped me not deal with the shock of seeing him in such a mess.

What I discovered that day, was that my brother was hooked on Nyaope[4]. We tried to get a rehabilitation centre that could take him without

4 Nyaope is highly addictive, the nyaope cocktail is made of heroin cut with methamphetamine, codeine and other substances reputedly ranging from anti-retroviral drugs to even powder from flat-screen televisions. It is smoked in a rolled joint laced with marijuana, or else liquidised and injected, it often leaves users with zombie-like sleepiness.

expecting an exorbitant fee, but the waiting lists were long. While he was sick, he was off the drugs. We nursed him to life. He stayed put for a while.

During that time, my grandmother passed away and two days before the funeral I discovered that my brother had no clothes as he had sold all of them. All he had was what he could not sell, basically torn clothes. I was heartbroken and yet again angry as a lot of those clothes were bought with my money. The furniture he had when he stayed on his own, was also gone.

I did not want to buy him anything, but as thick skinned as I usually am, I could not take the talks and the eyes behind my back. Again, I was angry at my family for telling me that I was not doing enough to take care of him.

I don't think I have ever displayed my anger publicly like I did on that day. How could they say that to me? I had to remind them that my brother was only two years younger than I, so he was not a child, but a fully-grown man. I had to remind them that I sacrificed my aspirations for his. Took care of him when I did not have to. Even so I still caved in and bought clothes for him, which he sold soon after the funeral.

Anyhow he soon disappeared from home after the funeral. He only came back a year later when he was ill, only this time, he was admitted to hospital. A few days later he passed away. Just like that, his end had come.

I felt cheated. I was devastated. I had always thought that one day he would find himself and dedicate his life to God. I was convinced that since he was a natural leader, he would one day be a soul winner for the kingdom. I had banked on his testimony being powerful, when he got saved. So, when he died I prayed for him to be resurrected. Mainly because I vacillated between anger, utter devastation and hope in that week of his burial.

One night I had a dream about him. In that dream he told me he did not want to come back, he said he was in a better place. This is when I remembered that each time he came back to his senses, he would apologise and accept Christ as Lord and saviour. Mainly because every friend that would have a 'one on one' conversation with him, would share the story of salvation with him.

Nothing in this world could have prepared me for his death. The pain of the loss was so unbearable that I could not breathe. From the moment we went to the hospital to arrange to move him from there to the morgue, I had entered into a state of shock. I had lost the ability to think beyond the here and now. It helped that Moruti Matshepo, my friend and pastor at the time, came along with me. Her calmness and her ability to ask questions that I had suddenly become incapable of asking helped. In a way she enabled me to focus on the job at hand. Although I was in pain, I had to start the painful job of organising his funeral.

I was confronted by the fact that I had not thought I would be the one burying him. It seemed natural to me that I would have been the first one to die, as I was older. I could not understand in which world this all made sense. I would wake up in the morning and feel like my inner parts were tearing in pain, then I would not be able to stand without falling back to bed. I would scream and just cry; every morning was similar. It would take me a while to get up, until I remembered to call out to God, "please carry me, I can't do this on my own."

I realised during these days that my friends are a blessing. It seemed there was always someone bringing me food or fetching me from my house so that I did not have to drive alone while I was running different errands. These moments were a blessing to me. Although I was fine once I woke up, once in a while I would have moments of searing pain that I could not see or breathe.

Of all days, Thursday, two days before his funeral

was the worst one. I can't remember why, but I remember a friend of mine singing for me while another prayed, because words could not console me. I felt lost. I wished my brother would have had a child, even if it was out of wedlock. I would at least have a living picture of him. I oscillated from being angry, sad, to feeling a deep sense of betrayal. I had so many unanswered questions about my brother's life.

We buried him and put the much dreaded finality to his death. After we buried him, I allowed myself to weep for him. I was inconsolable. I was grateful to my director, who allowed me a few more days off work after the funeral.

Weeks after his funeral, I still could not stop crying, it took me a while to overcome his death. For months on end I would see someone like my brother walking down the street and I would follow them, only to remember that it could not be him. One day I found myself calling after a stranger thinking he was my brother. I guess I had temporarily lost my mind.

In retrospect, my brother's funeral was painful, as I felt that he had died prematurely. Secondly, his death made me question the power of my prayers. I had prayed for God to deliver him from the life of oblivion. I had prayed for his deliverance from drugs and so many other things, but in the end he still died.

Nothing hits you like a moment when you blame the one you pray to, as your faith feels unhinged. Especially as in spite of how you feel, you know that there is no better place you can run to, than to Him.

Eventually I healed and had to deal with what the life of my brother meant to me. I now realise that I had centred my life on him. Perhaps unknowingly I had made him my life's mission. Losing my parents was difficult, but losing my brother was crippling. He was the only sibling I had. In spite of his faults, he was the most beautiful guy I knew. My brother was kind to a fault, nothing compared to his generosity. He gave even when he had nothing to give. Only because he did not want to see anyone suffering.

When I did not want to relate to my father's side of the family, he was the one who encouraged me to give them a chance. He would call me, to ask when last I visited them, and he would offer to accompany me to go see them. They had treated him so badly, yet he had this huge capacity to forgive. History did not matter to him, what mattered was how we lived.

I had to make peace with the fact that I would never understand why he had to die. Nevertheless, I had to accept his death and the fact that I would never see him again. I had to embrace the idea that I no longer had a brother.

After my brother died, I needed assurance that I belonged, as the sense of never belonging arose again. Yet again I was grateful for my friends. Not only did they carry me throughout my ordeal, they helped me bury my brother and made sure that I did not have to worry about certain things.

My friends also helped me to fight the lie, that I was left alone. To lose every member of your nucleus family can make you feel alone and lost. In those moments, I had to remind myself that I was not alone and would never be alone, as God would always be with me. I was grateful to Seipati who constantly reminded me that I had family.

Today when I remember my brother, I have a lot of beautiful things to remember. His smile, his larger than life personality and his kind heart. Most of all, because after we buried him, we took a lot of pictures, I remember those who carried me during that moment. This has ensured that I am able to remember his death and burial with a smile. I will always remember the people who surrounded me with love, God has given me a beautiful family.

CHAPTER 14

Detachment: although present,
I was absent

Out of the all the 'coping mechanisms' I developed; detachment was the worst of them all. It caught me off guard. Until the Holy Spirit revealed it, I did not even know that 'it was a thing'. Worse, the day I was given a glimpse of it, I was gobsmacked.

According to Wikipedia, detachment refers to an "inability to connect" with others emotionally, as well as a means of dealing with anxiety by preventing certain situations that trigger it. It is often described as "emotional numbing", "emotional blunting", or dissociation, depersonalization.

Yes, yes, I used Wikipedia. Please don't judge me this is not an academic journal, just my personal story. Now that we have that sorted let's get back to the matter at hand.

I was not 'an obviously' detached person, and neither was I completely disconnected to others emotionally. It was only in circumstances that caused me extreme emotional discomfort that the walls of detachment came up.

The trigger for detachment was always the need to protect myself. Sometimes I would disassociate from my emotions or I would numb myself from whatever I was feeling. I could walk away from a painful experience with a sad smile and not cry about the issue. The challenge was that even when I wanted to connect, I did not know how to.

As I said, I was not aware of this problem, until God brought to remembrance the times when detachment had affected how I related with people. Most of these experiences happened around mentors. Pretty much because in their environment, it was as if God held up a mirror where I could truly see myself as I was, not as I ordinarily deceived myself to be.

The one experience that came to mind when I was writing this book, was my first alone visit to my mentors' home. I had asked for a meeting as I was going through a spiritual crisis. I was struggling with God's calling concerning my prayer ministry. We settled for a Sunday afternoon meeting.

I think that I may have forced them into inviting me for a sleepover. Which was brave of me, given that I was never one for sleepovers. I pretty much had only ever slept over at houses of people I had known for a while and had quite grown comfortable with. The fact that I suggested this arrangement was beyond me, but I guess I was desperate.

Nothing would have prepared me for the kind of conversation that ensued. I had never had a 'one on one' conversation with Pastor Stella until that day. Although I had been acquainted with her for years, I had never been in a room alone with her.

Before I asked for a meeting with her, I felt God drawing me towards her and no matter how much I resisted, the pull was strong. When I found myself battling with my ministry of prayer and I did not know where to go, God directed me to her.

Until that fateful day I had always been able to deflect any personal question from Pastor Stella. Plus, it helped that the conversations I had with her prior to that day had always included other people. Typically, whenever a conversation got too personal I would avert, respond with humour or keep things at an intellectual level.

Anyhow I got there on time, and after all the pleasant hellos, our meeting started. I was then asked to get into my reason for being there. For the first time in my life, I found myself going from pillar to post. However, Pastor Stella's brilliance is her ability to help you to declutter and to focus on what is bothering you.

In all honesty I found her questions helpful and I appreciated her wisdom. What I did not anticipate was how our conversation would reach depths of my heart I had never allowed anyone to reach. By the time, Pastor Eddie arrived home our meeting was done. However, since he was into prayer we got talking about my plans with him. By then the conversation was light-hearted and very general in nature, but I freaked out. It seems Pastor Stella had managed to walk through my carefully constructed walls. I felt exposed, it felt like I needed to cover up. I was petrified and the more I thought of it, the more I struggled to pay attention to the current conversation. I was getting lost in my mind. I could not imagine spending any more time in that place. I felt apprehensive.

They told me about a prayer place nearby and when they saw my interest they asked if I wanted to go see it. I said yes, but as we were getting ready to go I decided that when we came back, I was going to drive back to Johannesburg.

You can imagine their surprise, but I did not care, all I wanted was to run as far away from them as possible. I wanted to put a barrier between myself and my emotions. On that day, I could not deflect or use humour to avoid answering or dealing with my emotions.

To date, I am grateful that my pastors are the people they are. They were able to forgive my rudeness and were gracious enough never to remind me of my behaviour. The realisation of how awkward I made things, was my inspiration to seek healing.

I needed to confront why I could not connect even when I wanted to. I had to tackle why being open with my true self, alarmed me. I realised that for me detachment was paired with control. Where I was in control, it was easier to connect. However, where there was no opportunity to control, I detached, as I thought being open posed a risk of being hurt.

Overcoming detachment is not an overnight thing. In therapy, I dealt with the root issues of detachment, which for me, were fear and the need to protect myself. The need to protect myself was a consequence of all the times I had been violated and felt I was not protected.

Additionally, I had to deal with the source of the desire to control which in my life was a great part of determining whether I let my guard down or not. An important note to be aware of is that all these things are connected. If I had not been not abused, I probably would not have had the need to protect myself by controlling situations or learning to detach from stressful environments.

Beyond therapy I had to intentionally walk the path of openness. I had to challenge myself whenever I saw myself closing up or being anxious. In those situations, I had to ask myself why I felt exposed and most importantly, question myself about what is wrong with being exposed. That often revealed the source of my fear, which then helped me to deal with it.

I also had to make myself aware that I am attempting to control things I should not be controlling, reminding myself that God is in control and He has me covered. Doing this has enabled me to overcome situations that used to make me anxious. I can't tell you how many, times I have had to remind myself to relax.

Today my life is open, and I deliberately work at keeping myself open and vulnerable. When I see myself hardening my heart or numbing my feelings because I can't cope with my immediate environment or intense emotions, I command my body be calm. I also often pray for courage to feel what I have to feel, and to work through it one step at a time.

CHAPTER 15

The state of sunshine

I don't quite know how I survived what I lived through. Now that I remember most of the things that I have gone through, I see the hand of God in my life. I am amazed that I have turned out this well.

The more we unpacked and peeled off the layers and the different personalities I had created, the more I wondered whose life I had lived all along. I wonder how I had survived. It feels like my life had been held together by a thin cotton thread that could have easily been torn, had God not strengthened it. I am sure there are a lot of explanations that we could come up with, but I know the degree of my brokenness. I am convinced that it is only God who could have carried me through.

There were so many opportunities to give up, be bitter or be resentful, but God protected me from all of these. Even when I had plans to do evil, he still protected me from myself and from inflicting harm. Without God I would not have been able to heal from my past.

I had spent so much of my past wondering why satan hated me so much. But seeing what I was able to achieve even in my state of brokenness, I understand why he had to try to make me give up on life. I am certain that he did not bargain for me making it my life goal to free others who are held in bondage like I was.

I have met a lot of broken people, some because they were rejected or abused as children. Whatever has caused you harm, I want you to know that God has availed His healing for you.

It is important to note that living in a fallen world, means people can behave like animals and hurt each other in incomprehensible ways. It is a horrible thing that they do that. Most often when we experience that we question the God who created them, as if he is responsible for their evil choices. Trust me, a good God cannot create evil people, but a fallen world can turn good people into pure evil.

Indeed, in writing this book, there are a lot of things or experiences I did not share. As it is hard to choose what to share and what not to share, as it's impossible to narrate every detail of one's life. However, I hope I have shared enough to show you that no matter how horrible your life may be, or has been, God can heal and free you.

Often we tell the story of letting go or getting rid of a painful scar, but part of healing is learning to walk without the scar. This is the story we never tell. It's amazing how scars become disabilities that we begin to identify with, taking them as part of who we are. While I was happy that I was free, I had to deal with what it meant in practice. I have had to repeatedly adopt the person that was being revealed, after the layers were peeled off. This was often scary as this person was a stranger. This stranger who was the new me being unearthed, often made me uncomfortable, and a few times I wanted to run very far from her.

I had to learn to get re-acquainted with the self that was emerging. It was also necessary to re-introduce this new self to those around me, otherwise people responded to the old me, which made maintaining the gains I had received, difficult.

Sometimes I got frustrated as I wanted immediate

answers, but I learned to be patient with myself and to allow God to help me find my true self. I had to learn to meet be with myself without placing expectations or judging a behaviour I was unfamiliar with.

Sometimes my reaction to certain things would shock me as it would be contrary to whom I thought myself to be. In these moments, it was crucial to allow myself to be, without trying to subvert the emerging person.

I have learned that sometimes it is possible to heal from a thing only to be drawn back to your old self. This happened to me a few times. I suppose the rapidness of change must have been so swift and uncomfortable, that there was sometimes a temptation to go back to what I knew.

In those moments when I regressed I had to know that I did not need to seek healing again, as it was already granted. What I needed to do was to remind myself that I was healed, set free and delivered. Then I had to engage with why I was pulled back into my past.

Since brokenness is comfortable and gives you an excuse not overcome, it's important to teach yourself not to behave like you are still broken, or not to use the excuses that you have. Only you can close the door to your brokenness. You need to learn to re-define what characterises you and how that is expressed through your habits.

This is important, as I was so shocked when a strong woman emerged out of me. This powerful woman who was a bulldozer, scared me enough that I wanted to suppress her at all costs. When this happened in a matter of weeks, I found old things that I had dealt with threatening to take over again. I was losing my gains. Thankfully, going to therapy had equipped me with tools of healing; so soon enough I stopped my trajectory, and reversed my losses.

To change the pattern, I needed a conversation with myself to check why this was happening. Once I found out, I dealt with it. The lesson for me in this is that healing is a continuous journey. Until you have fully established good thinking patterns and foundational truths that cannot be shaken, your past remains a threat.

Life is a beautiful journey with beautiful experiences. We can either intentionally create them or we can assume that we will accidentally come upon them and be passive participants of our life journeys. For the longest time, I was a passive participant of my life but now I refuse to be. I want every experience and every encounter, to count. After all, my life is purposed by God and its worth living.

I want my life to count for something. I want to impact lives and give hope. I am convinced that the idea that I would make it somehow, which consumed me throughout my childhood, is what kept me going. I am persuaded that this is what I have come to call hope.

I laugh the hardest and the loudest, because I appreciate the happiness that this brings to my life. I don't spend a lot of time angry or sad, as I know this is a waste of precious time. This is why I spend a lot of time praying for myself, particularly my emotional wellbeing, as I know that being happy is a choice I have to make every day.

I hope I have encouraged you to seek your own healing.

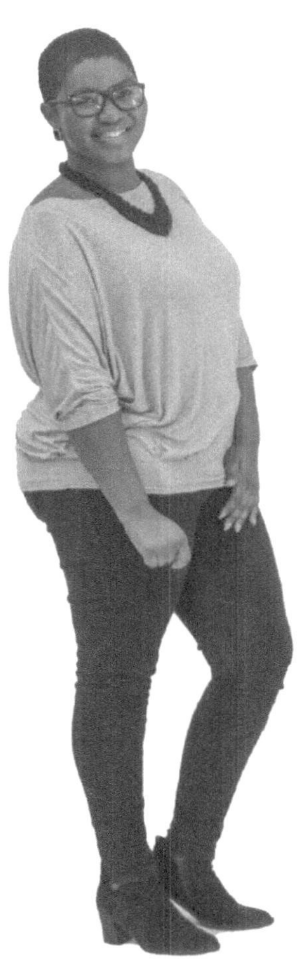

KHUMO
BOOKS